Planning the Curriculum for Pupils with Special Educational Needs

2nd Edition

Other titles of interest:

A Sensory Approach to the Curriculum
for Pupils with Profound and Multiple Learning Difficulties
Judy Davis
1–85346–671–9

Towards a Curriculum for All
A Practical Guide for Developing an Inclusive Curriculum for Pupils Attaining Significantly
Below Age-Related Expectations
Dorchester Curriculum Group
1–85346–773–1

Inclusion and School Improvement
A Practical Guide
Rita Cheminais
1–84312–005–4

First Steps in Inclusion
A Handbook for Parents, Teachers, Governors and LEAs
Stephanie Lorenz
1–85346–763–4

The SENCO Handbook (4th Edition)
Working Within a Whole-School Approach
Elizabeth Cowne
1–84312–031–3

Planning the curriculum for pupils with special educational needs

A pra[ctical]

Chapt.
7.
10.

Second

Richa[rd]   [R]ose

Uprima®

David Fulton Publishers

David Fulton Publishers Ltd
The Chiswick Centre, 414 Chiswick High Road, London W4 5TF

www.fultonpublishers.co.uk

First published in Great Britain in 2004 by David Fulton Publishers

10 9 8 7 6 5 4 3 2 1

Note: The right of the authors to be identified as the authors of this work has been
asserted by them in accordance with the Copyright, Designs and Patents Act 1988.
David Fulton Publishers is a division of Granada Learning Limited, part of
Granada plc.

British Library Cataloguing in Publication Data
A catalogue record for this book is available from the British Library.

ISBN 1 85346 779 0

Typeset by RefineCatch Limited, Bungay, Suffolk
Printed and bound in Great Britain

Contents

Acknowledgements

We wish to dedicate this book to practitioners, with many thanks for affording us the privilege of sharing in your classroom processes and development tasks. The contents of this book belong, in many senses, to you, as you will recognise. We acknowledge in particular, Amwell View School, Stanstead Abbots; Brooke School, Rugby; Durants School, Enfield; Dycorts School, Romford; Falconer's Hill Infants School, Daventry; Glenwood School, Dunstable; Grange School, Bedford; Greenfields School, Northampton; Greenside School, Stevenage; Heritage House School, Chesham; Hillcrest School, Dunstable; Jack Taylor School, Camden; John Smeaton Community High School, Leeds; Lancaster School, Westcliff-on-Sea; Lidgett Grove School, York; Meldreth Manor School (SCOPE), Royston; Montacute School, Poole; Pen y Cwm School, Ebbw Vale; Rees Thomas School, Cambridge; Rutland House School (SCOPE), Nottingham; St George's School, Peterborough; St John's School, Bedford; Watling View School, St Albans; Woodlands School, Chelmsford; the Northamptonshire Special Schools; staff in the Learning Support Services and schools in the London Borough of Newham; all the countless participants in staff development sessions provided by 'the two Richards' and other teams of teachers who have influenced our thinking over the years.

In addition, we wish to acknowledge the support of the University of Cambridge Faculty of Education and the Centre for Special Needs Education and Research, University College Northampton. Thank you all, staff and students, for your interest and support.

Finally, we thank a number of individuals for their contributions to this volume: the irreplaceable Peggy Nunn for her help with the preparation of the manuscript; colleagues at David Fulton Publishers, for continuing support and patience; and Christina Tilstone for her *Foreword*.

Richard Byers and Richard Rose
October 2003

Foreword

When the first edition of *Planning the Curriculum for Pupils with Special Educational Needs* was published in 1996, reviewers regarded it as essential reading for school staff. It would, they maintained, enable schools to develop the curriculum collaboratively in order to identify strengths and weaknesses and to acknowledge collective achievements and successes. Both are vital elements that continue to be evident in this second edition, but the new material added by the 'two Richards' and their positive response to the radical, and often unpredictable, changes in education will also lead individual staff to a critical investigation of their own practices. The material includes, for example, information on the most recent guidance, notably the revised National Curriculum and the QCA *Guidance on Planning, Teaching and Assessing the Curriculum for Pupils with Learning Difficulties*, together with the updated *Special Educational Needs Code of Practice*.

This book, therefore, serves two important functions: it encourages the development of a relevant curriculum to meet the needs of pupils with a wide range of needs within the reconsidered legal framework; at the same time, it promotes what is referred to in Chapter 3 as 'self dialogue'. The content of each chapter ensures that such a dialogue is firmly embedded in school-focused and school-driven initiatives and is fundamental to the continuing professional development of each member of staff. 'School development' becomes 'teacher development' and, to this end, the two Richards do not prescribe set formulae, nor advocate specific courses of action. Rather, they have organised the book in such a way that excellent in-service strategies are provided which take into account the varying needs, expertise and experience of the individual. The selective readings and free-standing subsections, together with a rich range of practical examples, encourage members of staff to become reflective practitioners who can have confidence in their own skills in teaching and developing an appropriate curriculum for all pupils, including those with the most complex and challenging needs. Throughout it is stressed that the tried and tested ideas of the authors and the many teachers with whom they have worked, should be carefully considered, analysed and evaluated before being adopted by staff, taking into account the current state of curriculum development in their schools. The messages of engagement, dialogue and exploration are clearly set out in all sections and reflect the sentiments expressed in the proverb 'by learning you will teach; by teaching you will learn'. As a result, the book makes an important contribution to the development of the curriculum and to the professional self-evaluation and development of all members of staff.

Christina Tilstone
January 2004

The curriculum planning process

These pages do not contain a neat formula for producing paperwork. We believe that curriculum development is a process entailing a commitment to continuous review and renewal. We do, it is true, argue for phased renewal, so that some of the stages of the development process we describe may produce outcomes that can be formalised into carefully presented curriculum documentation which will remain in use in the long and medium terms. We also make it clear that other aspects of the curriculum planning process must remain short-term, responsive, subject to constant revision, characterised by hastily composed working papers and swift mental reactions, if they are truly to acknowledge changing priorities for individual pupils.

This book does not present a single answer to any of the questions it poses. Rather it calls upon staff who work with pupils with special educational needs in a range of educational settings, all of whom make individual responses to a sense of common challenge, to use their wealth of experience in order to generate a variety of responses. We cherish the diversity of these outcomes and have tried to represent as wide a range of possibilities as we can in the following pages. We offer worked examples of sheets and, in many cases, blank formats that you can copy for your own use. You may find some ideas that you can pick up and use much as they are. We hope you will prefer to adapt before you adopt, tailoring ideas to the current state of curriculum development in your school.

We recognise that not all schools will wish to proceed from first principles. We have therefore designed this book for selective reading, with sections and subsections that are free-standing but, we hope, usefully cross-referenced. The detailed contents page will help you to find your way through the text. Our contention is that you may wish to start halfway through the book now – but that you will need to come back to all its sections at some point in the curriculum planning process in your school.

Aspects of the curriculum planning process

If you follow the sections of this book in sequence, you will move from a review of breadth, balance and the allocation of time within the whole curriculum in Chapter 2 to Chapter 3, which is designed to contribute to policy-making and review in relation to both National Curriculum subjects and other aspects of the whole curriculum.

Chapter 4 deals with the broad sweep of long-term planning in relation to the programmes of study for the National Curriculum. We draw a distinction between continuing work and discrete units of work and consider aspects that merit being taught in depth and those that schools may decide to cover in outline. We review the process of planning through year groups and between departments, and advocate documentation that outlines content and coverage in terms of programmes of study and key stages. We encourage schools to identify and capitalise upon the links between units of work in order to promote coherence. We do not consider it useful to prescribe a time period that may be considered 'long term'. Clearly, planning at this level deals with departments, key stages and year groups rather than days or weeks, but it is perhaps more helpful to think of this phase of the planning process as strategic, likely to lead to documents that are formalised and semi-permanent, the first stage in translating policy into practice.

Chapter 5 describes the formulation of medium-term plans through units of work and modules that identify areas of work to be covered over a term or half a term. Here we suggest that defining strands of subject content through sequences of proposed activity will enhance progression and continuity. We argue that subject-focused teaching should be clarified, in medium-term plans, by the identification of objectives for learning and the exemplification of activity at each age stage. Planning, we emphasise, should also anticipate the assessment opportunities, integral to teaching and learning, that classroom activity founded in subject-focused schemes of work will present. Plans at this level may be formal but will be subject to more frequent review and revision than long-term plans.

In Chapter 6, we deal with short-term planning and decisions to be made about classroom activity on a detailed session-by-session, week-by-week basis, at least during the development phase as staff build up a 'library' of teaching ideas. We discuss classroom processes and methods, including the integration of individual targets into group activity, and planning for differentiation by accounting for a range of possible prior levels of pupil interest and achievement. We also discuss pupil groupings and resource issues concerning location, staffing, equipment and materials. We acknowledge that short-term plans are likely to be informal, ephemeral, individual and subject to continuous revision in the light of circumstances during implementation. For experienced teachers they may also be more thought-through than written down; more jotted notes than typeset document.

In Chapter 7 we focus on individual education planning. We propose, with the *Special Educational Needs SEN Code of Practice* (DfES 2001a), that another aspect of short-term planning involves target setting or establishing short-term priorities for individual pupils. We suggest that these targets will be derived from annual aims or clusters of objectives and may be negotiated with pupils, parents and other professionals. Whether targets are expressed in terms of either cross-curricular skills; or subject-specific skills, knowledge and understanding; or both, short-term planning will ensure that opportunities for making records and assessments occur and are made use of.

In discussing ways of monitoring pupil responses, we emphasise the distinction between recording experience and achievement. We suggest that records should take account of planned outcomes and incidental responses, noting progress in relation to both individual targets and group activity. We explore, in Chapter 8, methods of recording that are integral to teaching time, including pupil self-recording, and acknowledge a range of sources of evidence, including examples of work, photographs and video.

Our contention in this book is that all development is cyclical and moves through planning and implementation phases towards a process of review and evaluation. This process operates on a number of levels. Teacher and pupil records will contribute to assessment and reporting and to the review of individual progress in relation to targets and priorities. Staff may thus use carefully managed sampling strategies to monitor the effectiveness of individual teaching programmes while information builds up for annual reporting, annual review and the recording of achievement.

In Chapter 9, on curriculum co-ordination, we also highlight the importance of evaluating units of work themselves. This process will ensure, for example, that plans for assessment opportunities within particular activities are accurately linked to programmes of study or performance descriptions, whether National Curriculum levels or the P-scales (DfEE 1998, revised 2001; QCA/DfEE 2001a) provided for the assessment of pupils achieving below Level 1, and that work levels are appropriate, as part of the process of maintaining policy under regular review. In Chapter 10, we draw together some of the themes of this book; encourage schools to take control of their own curriculum development processes; and look towards a more inclusive future.

Table 1.1 gives a one-page summary of the schemes of work development process in note form. Table 1.2 provides a similar summary of the individual education planning process. These summaries are designed to be read side by side, since they describe parallel processes. They intersect and overlap at the stage where links are indicated and diverge again for separate but related assessment and reporting outcomes.

The legislative position

This edition of *Planning the Curriculum for Pupils with Special Educational Needs* emerges into a radically changed legislative and advisory landscape. The original National Curriculum (NCC 1989) has now been subjected to two major review processes (Dearing 1993a, 1993b; DfE 1995; DfEE/QCA 1999a, 1999b). Three major projects have considered and resolved a number of major issues relating to the education of pupils with learning difficulties within the National Curriculum (NCC 1992; SCAA 1996; QCA/DfEE 2001a). The Ofsted inspection framework has been revised and guidance on inspections in specialist and inclusive settings has been provided (Ofsted 2003). The *Special Educational Needs Code of Practice* is in its second incarnation (DfE 1994; DfES 2001a) and a Code of Practice relating to the requirements of the Special Educational Needs and Disability Act (Stationery Office 2001) informs schools and colleges about the anticipatory actions they must take in preparation for a more inclusive future. After a Green Paper (DfEE 1997) and a Governmental *Programme of Action* (DfEE 1998a), the DfES has launched statutory guidance on *Inclusive Schooling* for children with special educational needs.

This guidance (DfES 2001c) is statutory, which means that it 'must not be ignored'. It provides a positive endorsement of inclusion. The DfES states that this will mean that more pupils with special educational needs will be educated in mainstream schools – in fact, the guidance argues that 'most children with SEN can be included'. The guidance proposes that, with few exceptions, pupils without Statements are to be educated in mainstream schools and that a mainstream education should also be the starting point for discussion as decisions are made about placements for those with Statements. Schools and local education authorities (LEAs) will be required to take 'reasonable steps', rather similar to the 'anticipatory action' they will be expected to take in relation to the Special Educational Needs and Disability Act 2001, to include individual pupils with special educational needs in mainstream schools. This does not signal the end of special educational provision, however. The DfES guidance argues that the role of special schools must be developed in a more inclusive future and that, increasingly, mainstream and special schools will need to work together. In this way, special and mainstream schools and LEAs will be

Table 1.1 Developing schemes of work

Policy-making and preparing guidelines for teaching

- Undertake strategic planning for each aspect of the whole curriculum and allocate time.
- Prepare implementation guidelines.
- Allocate responsibilities and prepare timescales for monitoring, evaluation and review.

Long-term planning

- Define content and coverage in terms of programmes of study, key stages and age groups.
- Show aims in terms of knowledge, skills, concepts and attitudes to be promoted.
- Show the relationship between continuing work and discrete units or modules.
- Indicate links between subjects or opportunities to run units in parallel.
- Plan for progression and note time to be devoted to each unit.

Medium-term planning

- Define objectives for learning.
- Exemplify sequences of key activities for typical groups of pupils/students in each age group.
- Outline access issues, differentiation strategies, and teaching methods and list resources.
- Define assessment opportunities.

Short-term planning

- Plan activities in detail – session by session, week by week – for specific groups of learners.
- Differentiate activities for particular pupils/students and for groups of learners.
- Deploy staff and equipment.
- Plan opportunities to record and assess in relation to:
  - curricular objectives
  - performance criteria related to accreditation
  - individual pupil/student targets.

Link to individual education plans (IEPs)

- Integrate individual pupil/student targets (set in terms of key skills) into group activity.

Record responses

- Note planned and incidental progress in relation to individual targets and planned activity.
- Gather samples of work, pupil self-recording, photos, video etc.
- Monitor experiences and achievements.

Monitor, evaluate and review

- Monitor teaching and individual pupil/student responses; evaluate and review individual pupil/student targets; short-term plans; medium-term plans; long-term plans and policy.

Assessment and reporting

- Measure progress against assessment opportunities linked to programmes of study and performance descriptions (levels and P-scales).
- Build up information for annual reporting and for the ongoing evaluation and review of schemes of work and policy.

Table 1.2 Developing individual education plans

Identification and assessment

■ Specify the nature and extent of the pupil's/student's difficulties.

Annual review

■ Look back over the past year for evidence of progress and difficulties in priority areas.

■ Identify future needs in order to review provision and placement.

■ Update the Statement and/or the transition plan in consultation with pupil/student, parents and fellow professionals.

Long-term aims

■ In the light of the annual review, set out broad aims, goals and intentions for the year ahead.

■ Consider the whole curriculum in consultation with pupil, parents and fellow professionals.

Short-term targets

■ Select from this set of broad, long-term aims a small set of priority, short-term targets for the weeks ahead set in terms of key cross-curricular skills and/or subject-specific knowledge, skills and understanding.

■ In consultation with pupil/student, parents and fellow professionals, make these targets:

  – few in number (between three and six)

  – specific to the individual (extra or different from those for other pupils)

  – relevant to the pupil's/student's current priority needs

  – achievable and teachable within a timescale of five or six weeks.

■ Establish success and/or exit criteria – how will we know when targets have been achieved?

Link to medium-term and/or short-term curriculum plans and group activity

■ Consider how and when the IEP targets will be addressed.

■ Plan for recording, monitoring and assessment opportunities and for review.

Record responses

■ Note planned and incidental progress in relation to individual targets and planned activity.

■ Gather samples of work, pupil self-recording, photos, video etc.

■ Monitor experiences and achievements.

Evaluation and review

■ Review specific, short-term targets and individual responses on a continuous, ongoing basis.

■ Relate this review to long-term aims (once a term? twice a year? and at annual review) in consultation with pupil/student, parents and fellow professionals where possible.

Assessment and reporting

■ Measure progress against long-term individual aims.

■ Build up information for reporting at annual review, for records of achievement/progress files and for the ongoing evaluation and review of schemes of work and policy.

able, suggests the guidance, to 'remove barriers' to learning and participation for pupils with special educational needs. We hope that this book will contribute to this process.

The National Curriculum (DfEE/QCA 1999a, 1999b), in the meantime, has been revised to provide a more explicit rationale for the school curriculum based on two interdependent aims:

■ The school curriculum should aim to provide opportunities for all pupils to learn and to achieve.

■ The school curriculum should aim to promote pupils' spiritual, moral, social and cultural development and prepare all pupils for the opportunities, responsibilities and experiences of adult life.

These aims are informed by a set of explicit purposes for the National Curriculum which state that education is a route to the spiritual, moral, social, cultural, physical and mental development, and thus the well-being, of the individual. Further, education is also seen as a route to equality of opportunity for all, a healthy and just democracy, a productive economy and sustainable development. These purposes are underpinned by a set of 'common' and 'enduring' values that contribute to these educational outcomes. These values entail 'valuing ourselves, our families and other relationships, the wider groups to which we belong, the diversity in our society and the environment in which we live'. According to the National Curriculum (DfEE/QCA 1999a, 1999b), education 'should also reaffirm our commitment to the virtues of truth, justice, honesty, trust and a sense of duty' and enable us to be responsive – for example, to 'economic, social and cultural change'; the 'globalisation of the economy and society'; 'new work and leisure patterns'; and the 'rapid expansion of communication technologies'.

On a more practical level, the National Curriculum for 2000 is both more flexible and more internally consistent than its predecessors. In particular:

■ The revised programmes of study for the core and non-core foundation subjects of the National Curriculum are less prescriptive.

■ Each subject has a single set of teaching requirements.

■ There is greater coherence within subjects, between subjects and with other initiatives, such as the National Strategies for Literacy and Numeracy (DfEE 1998b, 1999).

■ A common format is used for all subjects in all key stages.

■ A rationale is given for each subject.

■ Use of language across the curriculum is emphasised.

■ Use of information and communication technology across the curriculum is emphasised.

■ A new health and safety statement applies to science, design and technology, information and communication technology, art and design, and physical education.

■ Learning across the curriculum is enhanced in terms of:
   – spiritual, moral, social and cultural development;
   – key skills and thinking skills;
   – financial capability and education for sustainable development.

■ The National Curriculum provides, for the first time, non-statutory guidance for personal, social and health education (PSHE) and citizenship in all four key stages, with citizenship forming a statutory part of the curriculum in Key Stages 3 and 4 from August 2002.

■ Schools are offered greater flexibility in arriving at decisions about curriculum breadth and balance in Key Stage 4.

The drive towards consistency in presentation was seen as an important part of strengthening the National Curriculum. All programmes of study are now subdivided into key stages under the standard prefix 'pupils should be taught to ...' The process of rationalising the National Curriculum, however, also led to the removal of many of the references to teaching approaches. In general, the programmes of study now no longer describe the 'how' of teaching – working in groups, for instance – although this should not be seen as driving teaching in any particular methodological direction. We would argue that there is now an even greater need for teachers to consider and plan for a wide variety of approaches to teaching in order to encourage pupils to develop versatility in their repertoire of learning styles (Byers 1994a, 1994b; Babbage, Byers and Redding 1999).

Although overlap between subjects has, where possible, been removed, the review process has, in many senses, strengthened the links between different aspects of the curriculum. Many facets of the curriculum are given cross-curricular significance, and the key skills and thinking skills are described as 'universal' in their relevance. The important role that PSHE plays across the curriculum and beyond school is also acknowledged.

In terms of assessment, progression and continuity have been highlighted through improved 'stranding' in all the subjects. The assessment scale, with eight smoothly progressive levels, has been enhanced with the provision of a scale for 'exceptional performance' and supplementary P-scales for pupils achieving below Level 1 (QCA/DfEE 2001a). The original Dearing review (Dearing 1993a, 1993b) resulted in a profound shift away from statements of attainment to level descriptions. This should mean that tick-list driven teaching, focused solely on assessment outcomes, is no longer appropriate. As SCAA (1994) states:

> ... it is the programmes of study which should guide the planning, teaching and day-to-day assessment of pupils' work. The essential function of the level descriptions is to assist in the making of summary judgements about pupils' achievements as a basis for reporting at the end of a key stage.
>
> (p. 6)

Teachers no longer need to make complex, mechanistic calculations about scores in relation to individual fragments of pupil achievement. Instead they should use their professional judgement, based on a range of forms of evidence including samples of work and their own observations, in deciding which description 'best fits' the whole of a pupil's performance at the end of a key stage.

An inclusive curriculum

The revised National Curriculum places a strong emphasis on providing effective learning opportunities for all learners and establishes three principles for promoting inclusion. These principles challenge practitioners in inclusive settings to:

■ Set suitable learning challenges.

■ Respond to pupils' diverse learning needs.

■ Overcome potential barriers to learning and assessment for individuals and groups of pupils.

The inclusion statement is designed to help staff to meet the needs of all pupils and there are specific notes, for example, to help staff who work with pupils with disabilities and pupils who are learning English as an additional language. In order to have due regard to these principles for pupils with special educational needs, the National Curriculum suggests that staff may need to:

■ Differentiate tasks and materials.

■ Work with other agencies.

■ Facilitate access to learning by:
   – providing help with communication, language and literacy;
   – encouraging pupils to use all available senses and experiences;
   – planning for full participation in learning and in physical and practical activities;
   – helping pupils to manage their behaviour, to take part in learning and to prepare for work;
   – helping pupils to manage their emotions.

These changes go a long way towards resolving difficulties over chronological age and key stage. The review teams working on the revisions to the National Curriculum were asked to write programmes of study in such a way that pupils could demonstrate achievement at the earliest levels in all key stages. Where necessary, school staff are also given the discretion to teach pupils material from earlier (or later) key stages without recourse to formal modification or disapplication procedures, providing due consideration is given to age-appropriate learning contexts. This means that a 14-year-old pupil with profound and multiple learning difficulties can be taught those aspects of the programmes of study for science at Key Stage 3 that are relevant and that can be rendered accessible while at the same time continuing to work on suitable material founded in the programmes of study for Key Stage 1. Stevens (1995) makes it clear that staff should look to the programmes of study devised for a pupil's chronological age *first* in their planning and that disapplication procedures must still be followed where it is deemed to be impossible to devise routes of access to an entire area of study, regardless of key stage.

At the same time, the revised *SEN Code of Practice* (DfES 2001a) highlights the importance of planning to meet the individual needs of young people, both through school action and through approaches that involve parents and collaboration with other professionals. A cyclical process of planning, target setting and review should ensure that the priority needs of these young people are met within school and through the curriculum. The issues addressed in this process will not be limited to the subject content of the school curriculum, however. As we will emphasise later in this book, individual education planning will focus on a wider range of issues of direct relevance to the needs of pupils, including medical, paramedical and therapeutic issues, the development of key skills, and personal and social growth.

Taken together, these ideas mean that schools can take a genuinely integrated approach to pupils' learning. It should now be possible to ensure that medical or therapeutic priorities, as well as teaching and learning focused on essential key skills and the development of the whole pupil, can be addressed alongside, in the context of and in harmony with knowledge skills and understanding drawn from the subjects of the National Curriculum. We hope to exemplify many of these principles in action

Figure 1.1 Enabling access

In the course of all schemes of work, this school will endeavour to maintain the conditions most likely to facilitate learning for all pupils through:

- the provision of appropriate information technology hardware, software and peripherals;

- the correct use of positioning and mobility aids;

- the observance of therapeutic regimes of all kinds – whether based in speech therapy, physiotherapy or medication;

- the implementation of strategies to alleviate sensory impairments;

- the consistent and sensitive application of programmes designed to moderate challenging behaviours;

and through a commitment to interdisciplinary collaboration and partnership with parents, fellow professionals, pupils and the community of which we are a part.

Many of the teaching activities exemplified in these schemes of work derive from programmes of study for Key Stage 1. These activities have been carefully developed to provide continuity, progression and age-appropriate learning contexts for pupils seeking achievement at the earliest levels across the age range.

Other activities are founded in programmes of study for Key Stages 2, 3 and 4 and offer pupils access to relevant, age-appropriate material both at earlier levels and beyond. Some aspects of the programmes of study for the later key stages are liable to remain inaccessible or irrelevant for some pupils.

These schemes of work present a considered view of the breadth and depth of study appropriate to pupils at this school. However, individually targeted programmes are provided for all pupils, including those at either end of the spectrum of achievement.

Many pupils will need to revisit fresh interpretations of Key Stage 1 material throughout their school careers. For some, the challenge of achievement will prove problematic. In extreme cases, certain aspects of this work will remain inaccessible for particular pupils. In these instances, pupils' individual Statements will reflect the situation.

There will be other pupils whose studies will lead them beyond the scope of the material represented in these schemes of work. In all such cases we offer individually differentiated enrichment activities, based on these schemes of work, upon other related aspects of the programmes of study for Key Stages 1, 2, 3 and 4, and upon other priorities within the whole curriculum.

in the pages of this book. Figure 1.1 gives an example of the kind of access statement that schools can now offer as a preamble to schemes of work documentation. This wording has been developed in an all-age school for pupils with severe and profound and multiple learning difficulties and it reflects the potential achievements of these pupils as perceived by the staff. The statement could be adapted for use in other settings.

Closing comments

The changes we have reviewed briefly here have resulted in greatly increased flexibility of access; wide discretionary powers for teachers and schools in planning activity that is relevant and meaningful to all pupils; and a rounded view of assessment with no further need for the mechanistic checking off of isolated performance indicators. These are profound changes indeed – changes which, as this book will explore, have particular resonance for pupils with special educational needs.

We hope that teachers, senior managers, subject co-ordinators and members of school support staff will be interested in this book and find its content practical and useful. It may also help governors, parents and other professionals who participate in the curriculum development process. We are confident that the ideas we present in the following chapters will be applicable for pupils with a range of special educational needs, in special schools and in inclusive mainstream settings.

In writing this book we have deliberately sought to build on the ideas and practical approaches set out in previous volumes, such as *Redefining the Whole Curriculum for Pupils with Learning Difficulties* (Sebba, Byers and Rose 1993, revised 1995) and *Implementing the Whole Curriculum for Pupils with Learning Difficulties* (Rose, Fergusson, Coles, Byers and Banes 1994, revised 1996). We therefore follow similar conventions in attempting to avoid gender stereotyping and the unnecessary labelling of pupils. However, where the examples we offer relate to a specific group of pupils, we have, for the sake of clarity, identified, for instance, moderate or profound and multiple learning difficulties. Readers should be aware that the precise definition of such categories will vary from school to school and from authority to authority. Our use of these terms should therefore be seen as a general guide to levels of access. We do, in any case, seek to broaden the debate where possible to emphasise the inclusion of a wide range of pupils who experience individual educational needs. We believe that the issues we raise in this book have relevance across that range of need and, indeed, beyond. The principles we wish to celebrate here are principles of good practice and it is not our intention to limit their application to any narrow or artificial section of the school population.

Establishing principles

2

The whole curriculum

The activities proposed in this chapter can be seen as a preparation for the work on policy-making we present in Chapter 3. They will lay some foundations for the long-term and medium-term planning tasks we describe in Chapters 4 and 5. The discussion these activities will engender will also help to clarify a way forward for curriculum development teams already engaged in policy-making and planning in relation to a range of aspects of the whole curriculum. The activities can be used to summarise and review work already undertaken and to set that work in the context of a revitalised debate about curriculum breadth and balance. This revitalised debate has been made possible by the publication of a revised National Curriculum (DfEE/QCA 1999a, 1999b) and a range of other items of guidance and advice designed to promote the inclusion of pupils with special educational needs in shared learning opportunities while securing their entitlement to receive an education that addresses their individual needs. *Planning, Teaching and Assessing the Curriculum for Pupils with Learning Difficulties – General Guidelines* (QCA/DfEE 2001a) makes reference to these dual imperatives and suggests that schools need to take account of a number of issues when establishing a curriculum for particular communities of learners. These issues may include:

- their own school aims
- the needs of the pupils attending the school (which will change as they progress and grow older)
- the requirement to provide a broad and balanced curriculum (which includes the subjects of the National Curriculum and religious education)
- the national frameworks for teaching literacy and mathematics (which include the expectation of a daily dedicated literacy hour and daily mathematics lesson of 45 to 60 minutes)
- the needs of the local community.

(p. 12)

The QCA/DfEE (2001a) guidelines state that 'each school is responsible for determining the curriculum so that provision carefully matches local and individual circumstances' and that the revised National Curriculum should be seen, by staff, as providing a 'starting point for discussion' rather than a predefined set of imperatives (p. 6). The guidelines do, however, provide further detail about those aspects of the curriculum that form shared entitlements for all pupils in various age groups and which therefore need to be included in any curriculum for pupils with special educational needs. These elements include:

- *Curriculum Guidance for the Foundation Stage* (DfEE/QCA 2000) for pupils in the first years of their education
- the general requirements in the revised National Curriculum and, in particular, the statement on inclusion which sets out the requirements under three broad principles
- the full range of subjects of the National Curriculum, including citizenship at Key Stages 3 and 4 from 2002, religious education, sex and relationship education, other aspects of PSHE, and careers education, according to the relevant key stage
- provision which prepares pupils for adult life, with access to suitably accredited courses as they grow older.

(p. 7)

The expectations in relation to the national strategies for literacy and numeracy have been noted above. The statutory requirements in relation to the teaching of the core and non-core foundation subjects are summarised below:

- English, mathematics, science, design and technology, information and communication technology, and physical education are statutory across all four key stages.

- History, geography, and art and design are statutory across Key Stages 1 to 3.

- Modern foreign languages and citizenship are statutory in Key Stages 3 and 4.

Schools are also required to teach religious education and sex education, unless parents decide to withdraw their children, and careers education during Years 9, 10 and 11.

It should be noted that there is an expectation that schools should 'aspire' to provide two hours of physical activity each week, comprising physical education as set out in the National Curriculum together with extra-curricular activities, for all pupils in all key stages.

It should also be noted that schools are now required to make modifications to programmes of study in order to promote access for pupils with special educational needs. These modifications might include, in terms of the National Curriculum inclusion statement we discussed in Chapter 1, extensions to the programmes of study for particular subjects. Staff might wish to provide additional literacy work using symbols, for example, or break early mathematical learning down to promote notions of one-to-one correspondence or 'more' and 'less'.

The National Curriculum *Handbooks* (DfEE/QCA 1999a, 1999b) also make it clear that schools may also promote other aspects of the curriculum, drawing upon the cross-curricular elements that were identified in *Curriculum Guidance 3: The Whole Curriculum* (NCC 1990). These aspects include:

- financial capability – designed to help pupils make independent and informed decisions about managing money – keeping it safe, budgeting, spending, saving, sharing, borrowing and obtaining value for money

- enterprise education – designed to enable pupils to develop confidence, self-reliance and risk management skills through involvement in mini-enterprises

- education for sustainable development – designed to equip pupils to participate in decisions about the relationships between quality of life for people now and damage to the environment and the planet.

Pupils are also entitled to receive an education that helps them to 'acquire, develop, practise, apply and extend their skills in a range of contexts' (QCA/DfEE 2001a). These important skills will apply 'across the curriculum' and 'will also be relevant to life and learning outside and beyond the school'. Again according to QCA/DfEE (2001a), drawing upon the National Curriculum *Handbooks* (DfEE/QCA 1999a, 1999b), these skills include:

■ the key skills of communication (including literacy), application of number, information technology, working with others, improving own learning and performance and problem solving

■ thinking skills (including information processing, reasoning, enquiry, creative thinking and evaluation).

(p. 7)

The QCA/DfEE (2001b) guidance on *Developing Skills* suggests ways in which these skills may be interpreted and implemented for pupils with special educational needs and proposes further categories of important skills which individual pupils with learning difficulties may also need to develop. These include:

■ physical, orientation and mobility skills

■ organisation and study skills

■ personal and social skills, which include personal care and health skills, managing own behaviour and emotions

■ daily living skills, which include domestic and community skills

■ leisure and recreational skills.

(p. 14)

These skills will play an important part in the curriculum for all learners and perhaps particularly for pupils with special educational needs. They may be taught directly through group activities and opportunities to develop them can be highlighted in schemes of work for a range of subjects. As we show later in Chapter 7, we also suggest that they may also be prioritised and addressed in focused ways for specific learners through targets in individual education plans.

Many commentators have noted the particular significance of many of these ideas for pupils with learning difficulties (Ashdown, Carpenter and Bovair 1991; NCC 1992; Sebba, Byers and Rose 1993). Others would argue that there are yet other aspects of the discretionary curriculum that are of particular relevance to pupils with special educational needs and which merit a place within the whole curriculum (Ouvry 1991) – riding for the disabled, residential trips, lunch-time clubs and community links might be examples of such ideas.

Individual schools will be aware that the characteristic special educational needs of particular pupil populations will generate further curricular priorities. These may include an emphasis upon literacy skills where significant numbers of pupils have English as a second home language; time devoted to physiotherapy for pupils with physical disabilities or to language and communication therapy where pupils have severe learning difficulties; or opportunities for counselling and guidance for pupils who experience emotional and behavioural difficulties.

The whole notion of individual pupil priorities is central to effective curriculum planning. The *SEN Code of Practice* (DfES 2001a) emphasises the importance of the individual education plan, developed and monitored through the annual review procedure, for pupils with Statements of Special Educational Need. As has been clearly demonstrated (Ainscow 1989; Sebba, Byers and Rose 1993), schools need to balance the whole curriculum in response to pupils' individual needs.

Negotiating curriculum content

The National Curriculum is now properly seen as part of a 'broad statutory framework' within which schools are encouraged to 'create and pursue their own vision' (Tate 1994). Curriculum development is once again part of the school development agenda (Byers and Rose 1994).

Whether you are embarking on a review of the curriculum from first principles or pausing in an established process in order to take stock of progress so far, it may be useful to use the following activity to confirm or to renegotiate your school community's 'own vision' of curriculum content and to reappraise the ways in which your school timetable balances the complex demands of breadth and relevance.

Figures 2.1 and 2.2 can be copied onto card and cut up for use as a card game to promote whole-staff debate about curriculum content. Governors and parents have joined in with this exercise enthusiastically and constructively. Some cards are already printed with the titles of various aspects of the whole curriculum – subjects, themes and key skills – others are blank. Participants are dealt a hand of printed cards from a shuffled pack. Each player in turn selects a card from their hand and places it on the table, arguing a case for its inclusion in the school's whole curriculum. Players may comment about the role of each aspect and about the relationship between the ideas written on various cards. Comments and challenges from other players are to be welcomed.

Participants may swiftly decide that many of these aspects form part of the 'broad statutory framework' which Tate describes. They may move on to use the blank cards to make a case for including other aspects of the school's work within the whole curriculum as 'additional subjects', or particular school priorities. Players may call for extra sets of blank cards.

Schools catering for a broad age range of pupils will find that curriculum balance needs to be different in different departments or at different key stages. For younger children, for instance, exploratory play will be an important part of the curriculum and for the under-fives, for whom the National Curriculum does not apply, other curriculum categories may have a major role to play. Ofsted (2003) identifies six areas of learning for the under-fives:

- personal, social and emotional development
- communication, language and literacy
- mathematical development
- knowledge and understanding of the world
- creative development
- physical development.

At the other end of the spectrum, schools offering education for pupils with special educational needs post-16 will wish to consider a different range of priorities.

Ofsted (2003) suggests a series of 'curriculum areas post-16' that are consistent with those used in inspecting provision in colleges. These include:

- personal development and general programmes
- English, languages and communication
- mathematics, science, and information and communication technology
- humanities
- visual and performing arts, and media

Figure 2.1 Curriculum content card game

English	mathematics	science	history
geography	design and technology	information and communication technology	art and design
music	modern foreign languages	physical education	religious education
communication skills	application of number	working with others	problem-solving skills
improving own learning and performance	information technology skills	literacy	careers education and guidance
personal, social and health education	citizenship	numeracy	sex and relationship education

Figure 2.1 Curriculum content card game (continued)

financial capability	enterprise education	education for sustainable development	thinking skills

Figure 2.1 Curriculum content card game (continued)

and a series of options linked to vocational preparation: engineering, technology and manufacturing; hospitality, sports, leisure and travel; business; and health and social care.

School staff working with pupils within various key stages or age-related departments may wish to come to their own conclusions about the characteristic balance of content that is appropriate for their particular pupils. The curriculum for pupils with social and communicative difficulties in Year 5, for example, ought to be different from the curriculum offered to pupils with profound and multiple learning difficulties in their early teens. We would argue that this situation is made possible within the statutory framework and is actively promoted by the guidance.

Managing the whole curriculum

Having arrived at a set of preliminary responses to the question of what should be in the curriculum for various broad groupings of pupils at certain age-related stages in their school lives, schools will want to make decisions about how to manage these aspects of the curriculum and the relationships between them. We would argue that the whole curriculum for pupils with special educational needs is likely to be too complex to break down meaningfully into audited percentages of timetable time. A pupil with profound and multiple learning difficulties may be placed in her standing frame, and so receive a part of her physiotherapy programme, during a science lesson. A pupil on the autistic continuum may explore his feelings about his peer group, and so work towards one of his social development goals, during a class music session. Subtleties of this order will not be revealed in a simple audit of time allocation, especially since the precise nature of the balance within the whole curriculum must, we would argue, vary according to educational priorities for individual pupils as well as for groups of pupils in different age groups.

SCAA (1995) helpfully introduces a basic planning distinction between continuing work, which might be delivered in frequent, regular sessions or which permeates a range of different subject-related activities, and aspects of the curriculum that can be treated as separate, finite, distinct units of work. Staff may be encouraged to ask a series of questions about the aspects of the curriculum they identified in the previous activity:

- Which of these aspects require regular timetable slots?
- How frequent should these sessions be?
- Which aspects may be implemented in the course of other timetabled activities?
- Which aspects require occasional special arrangements?
- Which aspects should be seen as continuous, ongoing priorities?
- Which aspects can be treated as separate, discrete units of work?
- Are there links between certain aspects of the curriculum?

Curriculum development committees, which may include parents, fellow professionals and governors, will wish to respond to these and other questions about the management of the curriculum. Applying such questions to each aspect of the whole curriculum will lead departmental or key stage-specific teams towards agreements about the characteristic content, balance, flavour and delivery style of the curriculum for pupils at different age stages.

Considering different aspects of the whole curriculum in this way will thus produce a variety of outcomes. Whole-school, key stage or departmental teams will define the nature of the response they make for each aspect of the curriculum. The notes that are made should be retained. They will help schools to clarify the approach they wish to take in preparing to make policy and plans or in appraising progress in curriculum development to date. In the next chapter, we move on to discuss the process of making policy.

Making and applying policy

Every teacher in school is a manager. In their daily classroom practices, teachers have responsibility for the creation of an effective learning environment; the nurturing of pupils; leadership with regards to support staff, volunteers or students; and the management of the application of school policies, rules and regulations which contribute to the effective overall performance of the school. Without the necessary skills of management, or the appropriate planning structures, class teachers are unlikely to be able to support the school fully in achieving its objectives. Today's classrooms require teachers who are able to adjust to an ever-changing and increasing range of demands. Contemporary classrooms are places in which the traditional roles and responsibilities of staff are changing and established management hierarchies are blurred (Hall 1997). No matter how good the systems that are put into place in a school may be, it is only through their effective management by teams of professionals working together that the curriculum will achieve its objectives of meeting needs and establishing high standards in learning. Teachers now, more than at any time, need to demonstrate a level of initiative that enables the curriculum to be delivered in a flexible and considered way which addresses the needs of all pupils. As Morgan (1992) recognised:

> The importance of the human element in an organisation is increasing along with the pace of change. Change demands innovation, and innovation demands that we unleash the creative potential of our people. In a more stable world one could organise in a mechanistic way – establish and design one's organisation, direct and control it from the top, and rely on middle managers of fairly average ability to 'fill slots' with workers and oversee operations.
>
> Now, much more is required. Bureaucracy is giving way to new approaches that require people to exercise discretion, take initiative, and assume a much greater responsibility for their own organization and management. (p. 33)

It is apparent that much of the innovation in managing the curriculum for pupils with special educational needs which has been in evidence since the introduction of the National Curriculum has come from class teachers. This is hardly surprising, as it is class teachers who are responsible, on a daily basis, for devising and applying approaches that enable the pupils in their charge to progress, and who need to discover methods that will assist them in overcoming barriers to learning. Ainscow (1999, 2000) has suggested that effective class teachers engage in an intellectually demanding process of 'self-dialogue', constantly appraising their teaching approaches and challenging their own ideas, analysing those classroom actions that have been successful and reframing those that have not. Such a professional approach has proven to be essential as teachers have struggled to come to terms with the myriad curriculum changes and demands of recent years. It is this commitment that has often enabled teachers who are concerned for pupils with special educational needs to interpret, modify and improve upon those policies that have resulted from legislation which has all too often given inadequate consideration to the whole range of pupil needs.

In recent years, largely as a result of legislation, the development of policy has featured as a priority in many schools. Curriculum policies, special needs policies related to the *SEN Code of Practice* (DfE 1994; DfES 2001a) and other policies for aspects of school management have been established in most schools in all phases across the country. With one eye on the impending arrival of Ofsted (the Office for Standards in Education), schools have been concerned to put in place documentation that makes clear their philosophy and intentions, and this generally begins with the development of policy. If, however, the sole purpose of policy writing was to satisfy the requirements of agencies outside of school, it would be a thankless and largely futile task. Schools should defend their autonomy and their right to develop a philosophy which is unique to themselves. How often, in recent years, have schools hastened to adapt to new educational ideas only to find themselves forced to reconsider their position within a very short period of time? If policy has a purpose in school, it is in defining the individual characteristics that will enable the school to address most effectively the needs of its community – pupils, parents and staff (see Chapter 2).

Curriculum policy should, above all, be about schools influencing their own practice, ensuring consistency of approach and, where necessary, improving curriculum delivery. Policies should further be regarded as a means of communicating the aims and purpose of the school to those who have a vested interest – pupils, teachers, parents and the local community. The most effective policies are those that provide clear and unambiguous statements which can be easily interpreted and applied and can be used to have a direct influence upon the work of the school. Policies should be brief and should, of course, take account of legislation, and reflect the ethos and philosophy of the school.

The relationship between school development planning and policy development

The development of schools is dependent upon the establishment of priorities which are defined by those most closely concerned with their management and work. Development implies the improvement of practice and movement from a current position, where needs have been identified, to a new situation where changes made have a positive impact upon the school. Hargreaves and Hopkins (1991) state that:

> Development planning is about creating a school culture which will support the planning and management of changes of many different kinds. School culture is difficult to define, but is best thought of as the procedures, values and expectations that guide people's behaviour within an organization. The school's culture is essentially 'the way we do things around here'.
> (pp. 16–17)

The point made by Hargreaves and Hopkins is that each school is unique and, as such, is likely to establish its own working practices which will differ from those adopted by other establishments. In recent years, schools have invested considerable time in developing techniques that have enabled them to define their own priorities, and writers such as Reid, Hopkins and Holly (1987); Preedy (1992); Southworth (1993); and West-Burnham (1994) have provided models and advice which have encouraged schools to develop plans for effective development.

As schools have considered the need to become more inclusive and, in some instances, to address a greater range of pupils with special educational needs, self-review has played an increasingly important role in enabling schools to assess their readiness to elicit a more flexible response. The *Index for Inclusion* (Booth and Ainscow 2002) has found favour with practitioners and policy workers who have been concerned to ensure that the climate and ethos of the school and the systems in place for its management are supportive of the development of a more inclusive environment. Similarly, changes to the *Framework for Inspection* (Ofsted 2003) have encouraged school self-review and have enabled some schools to take a greater control of their own destiny when considering how they can adopt processes and implement policy to enable pupils with special educational needs to be more fully involved in all aspects of the curriculum and learning. While technocratic approaches alone will not ensure that schools provide a more effective curriculum to support pupils with special educational needs, the use of these forms of self-review must be welcomed as providing a starting point for schools wishing to become self-critical in respect of addressing the needs of all pupils.

It should be a matter of some concern that many schools are now reporting that their school development plans consist largely of priorities that have been provided by influences from outside of the school itself. The surfeit of legislation which has overtaken schools in the last ten years has led to the agenda for educational development being taken away from those who have the greatest investment in ensuring school success. School development plans are too often concerned with ensuring that the requirements of outside agencies, such as Ofsted, are going to be met and at times the needs of the school, as recognised by staff, governors and parents, are shelved in an effort to appease outside influences. Schools must regain control of their own destiny if staff are to be encouraged to tackle the important issues which relate directly to the needs of individual establishments. A tendency to regard the larger, national picture of education – as opposed to those matters which focus upon the school – has, in some instances, resulted in the postponement of the very development that would enable staff to become more effective in addressing the needs of their own pupil population.

This does not, of course, mean that schools should not be addressing national issues. It has been argued (Byers and Rose 1994) that those schools that maintain a principle of autonomy in the definition of priorities, also take on the added responsibility to ensure that, in so doing, the entitlement of all pupils to a curriculum that is balanced, broad, relevant and well differentiated is not jeopardised. It does, however, suggest that schools should be establishing their own priorities through school development planning which gives equal credence to local and internal matters. Policy is undoubtedly important for many of the reasons outlined above. This chapter is concerned to provide a practical model for development which may be used to address a wide range of policies, including those concerned with the curriculum.

A model for policy development

The relationship between policy and practice is an important one. It is through reference to policies that consistent practices should be achieved in schools. The notion that practice is wholly dependent upon policy is, however, a false one. In recent years it appears to have become fashionable to see policy as an essential driving force behind practice (see Figure 3.1).

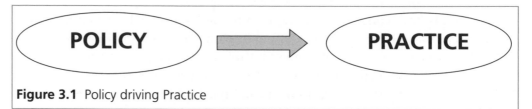

Figure 3.1 Policy driving Practice

Where this 'policy first' approach has been adopted, it has, in some instances, resulted in schools rejecting much of their existing practice in an effort to redefine where they are going. In this approach there is a risk that good practice, possibly established over a number of years, can be devalued and replaced with an altogether less satisfactory situation. Even in those schools where there are no written policies, there is generally a shared understanding of the way in which things are done. For example, a school may not have any written information about its lunch-time procedures, yet they may run smoothly, with all staff clear about their responsibilities and actions to be taken. When considering the writing of policies schools need to identify existing good practices and to build upon these, rather than trying to reinvent the wheel. This does not imply that schools should completely reverse the above approach, as in Figure 3.2.

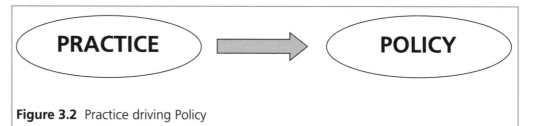

Figure 3.2 Practice driving Policy

Writing policy simply on the basis of existing practice denies an opportunity to review that practice and to look for where it may be improved or modified. A more useful approach is to aim for a synthesis between policy and practice (see Figure 3.3) in which policy is seen as an opportunity to review and build upon good practice, while making amendments and changes where necessary.

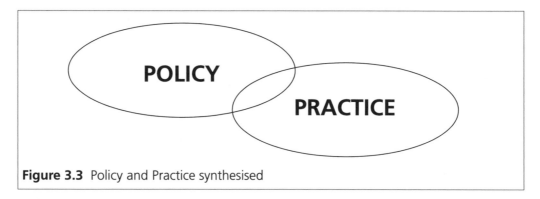

Figure 3.3 Policy and Practice synthesised

There is one approach to the development of policy, not uncommon in schools, in which one person, often the head or deputy, is charged with the responsibility for writing a document which is then distributed to staff for implementation. This does, of course, have certain advantages. Minimal time spent in discussion means that the policy is produced quickly, meetings are kept to a minimum and it is easy to achieve a consistency of style. There are, however, many pitfalls. The policy writer needs to be precise in the writing, in order that all staff can interpret its meaning without difficulty. A lack of staff participation means that total ownership by all staff may not be easily achieved. It may also result in any staff who disagree with the content of the policy feeling resentment, and applying it only with reluctance. Worst of all, it ignores staff expertise and experience, and does not provide opportunities for sharing in professional development.

An alternative approach entails involving all interested parties in policy development. This would seem to be ideal, but also has disadvantages and limitations. It is a lengthy and often difficult approach, and can make excessive demands upon an already busy staff. In a small school, staff may already be involved in several major projects, and have little time or inclination for attendance at additional meetings and researching other areas.

The model presented here provides a more effective approach which, while being consultative, also sets clear responsibilities and time lines. It accepts that there is a need to consult all interested parties and identifies times during the process when this consultation will take place. It also recognises policy development as a cyclical process, one in which the introduction of new ideas to the school, changes in legislation or changes in the school population can be recognised without a need for total reorganisation of the policy. The approach is based upon the cycle of development presented in Figure 3.4.

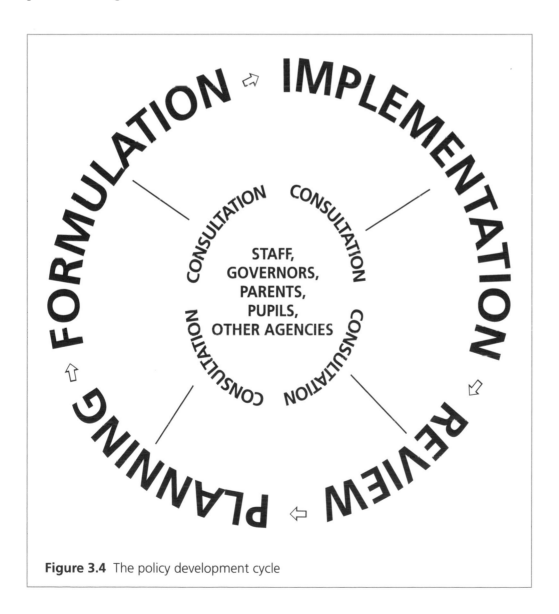

Figure 3.4 The policy development cycle

It should firstly be noted from this model that policy development is not seen as a 'once and for ever' process. It is ongoing and recognises the need for review which will, in turn, lead to modifications. The model recognises that schools are constantly evolving establishments and that, as change occurs, there is a need to adapt policy and procedures in order to address new issues and needs. In this model, the process of consultation with staff, governors, parents, pupils and other agencies is protected at every stage. This model is central to the practical approach to be described here.

Using the model

During the process of policy development, a policy map (see Figure 3.5) should be drawn up. This will provide the school with an indication of the actions to be taken to complete the writing and implementation of a policy. (Figure 3.10 gives a completed example.) The headings at the top of the columns on the policy planning map are used to indicate responsibilities, actions to be taken and timescale. The completed map is included here to give some indication of how it may look after each stage of completion. Please remember that this is only an example and does not suggest the way in which your school should allocate tasks or the timescale in which your school needs to work. The map must be used as a practical aid to development and should not dictate working practices to a school. When the map is complete, staff should have a clear idea about responsibilities and the timescale for developing the policy. Only at this point should the school begin to follow the map through to its conclusion with the production and implementation of a policy. The map should be completed by working through the activities for the four stages:

- Planning (P)
- Formulation (F)
- Implementation (I)
- Review (R).

Activity 1: the planning stage

This stage is concerned with establishing a purpose for the policy and identifying those persons who will be most closely concerned with its writing. It recognises the importance of consultation by establishing clear roles and responsibilities, not only for members of a working group but also for those persons to be consulted.

As you work through this stage, the row marked P (planning) will be completed. Complete this planning row by asking the questions at the head of the columns. Use the sheet provided (Figure 3.6) as a working sheet before entering details on your map.

1. Where are we now?

- Does the school have an existing policy in this area?
- Which current practices do we wish to retain which may be contained within the policy?
- Why have we decided that we need a policy?

2. Where do we want to be?

- When we have a policy, what will be its purpose?

Figure 3.5 Policy planning map

POLICY PLANNING MAP

School: Policy:

	Where are we now?	Where do we want to be?	What must we do?	Collective responsibility	My responsibility	Timescale
P						
F						
I						
R						

Figure 3.6 Policy planning stage activity

POLICY PLANNING STAGE ACTIVITY

At the beginning of the policy planning stage, work together as a staff to complete this chart. When you have finished this task, use the information to complete the **PLANNING** line of your policy map.

Why do we need this policy?	Who will be involved in developing the policy, and how?
What do we want the policy to contain?	How much time will it take?

- Why have a written policy?
- How will the situation in school have been improved by the writing of a policy?

3. What must we do?

- What methods will we deploy to construct our policy?
- How will we gather information?
- What guidance do we require from the school management or the local authority?
- What do we need to find out about this area for development?

4. What is the collective responsibility of people in the school community?

- What must staff, governors, parents, pupils and others do to help this process of development?

5. What is my responsibility?

- If I have a direct role to play in the development of the policy, what will it be and how can I help?

6. How long will it take?

- What other things are happening in school at present and during the immediate future?
- Do we have to time completion of this policy to coincide with a specific event (for example, a governors' meeting)?
- Which elements of the planning stage will take the greatest amount of time?

Time spent on the planning stage is critical and should avoid the necessity of redefining the working brief at later stages. During this stage, which is likely to involve a large number of people, concentrate only on planning. The greater detail of working practices can be established during the next stage, where fewer people are directly involved and therefore the process may be completed more quickly.

Activity 2: the formulation stage

During this stage you will complete the row marked F (formulation) on the planning map. Use the sheet (Figure 3.7) to make notes before entering details on the map. As in the planning stage, you need to ask a number of questions which will enable you to enter details in the formulation stage boxes. It is likely that at this stage you will

---

Figure 3.7 Policy formulation stage activity

POLICY FORMULATION STAGE ACTIVITY

When the planning stage of your policy map is completed, and you have established where you want to be, and assigned responsibilities, use this chart to provide information for the **FORMULATION** line of your policy map.

> List the contents of the document.

> Who will do what? How long will it take?

> Who and how will we consult?

> How will we communicate?

have a smaller number of people working directly on the task and that you should therefore be able to make good progress.

1. Where are we now?

- What has been decided about the way in which we will work?
- What brief has been established for the policy?

2. Where do we want to be?

- At the end of policy development, what will our policy look like?
- What will it contain?

3. What must we do?

- How will we work to achieve the requirements?
- How will we consult with others?
- How will we disseminate any information?
- How will we increase our understanding of this area?

4. What is the collective responsibility of people in the school community?

- Who has information which they must provide for the production of this policy?
- Who has ideas about its content?
- What needs to be read or examined?

5. What is my responsibility?

- What can I do to assist this process?
- With whom should I consult?
- What information do I already have?
- What do I need to find out?

6. How long will it take?

- What are the current commitments of the people involved at this stage?
- How often will people need to meet together?
- Which aspects of this stage will take the greatest amount of time?
- How will we make sure that everyone knows what the timescale of this stage is?

At the end of this exercise, it is essential that everyone concerned has access to the completed policy map and is clear about roles, responsibilities and timescale.

The formulation stage indicates the actions that will be taken to write the policy. The next stage is concerned with putting the policy into practice.

Activity 3: the implementation stage

During this stage, you will complete the row marked I (implementation). Use the sheet (Figure 3.8) for making your notes before completing the map. This stage is concerned with what will happen when the policy has been written, and how you will ensure that it is put into practice.

Figure 3.8 Policy implementation stage activity

POLICY IMPLEMENTATION STAGE ACTIVITY

When the formulation stage of your policy planning is completed, you need to ensure that the work carried out is implemented by all staff. Answer the questions on this chart, then complete the **IMPLEMENTATION** section of your policy map.

> Who needs to know about the new policy? How will we ensure that the policy we have written is understood?

> When will we begin applying the new policy?

> How will we know it is being implemented?

1. Where are we now?

At this point, you need to be clear that everyone concerned is familiar with the policy and its contents.

- Is the policy written in terms that are easily understood?
- Are sufficient copies available?
- Is the policy easily accessible to all who need to see it?

2. Where do we want to be?

- How do we intend that this policy should be used?
- Is the purpose of the policy clear?

3. What must we do?

- How will we disseminate information?
- Is there a need for training to ensure the implementation of the policy?
- Do we need to establish a system for monitoring the implementation of the policy?

4. What is the collective responsibility of people in the school community?

- What needs are there for changes in existing practice?

- Who will read the policy?
- Are expectations made clear?

5. What is my responsibility?

- Do I have to make changes to my practice?
- Can I assist others in the implementation of this policy?
- Can I identify my own training needs in relation to this policy?

6. How long will it take?

- Will we implement this whole policy at once or will we stagger its introduction?
- Are there resource implications which may affect the implementation of the policy?
- Do we need to take account of the time needed to train people prior to the implementation of the policy?

The final stage of this process is review. There is a danger that schools, having written a policy and implemented it, then move on to another project without considering the importance of review. Policies need constant review, but it is probable that the first time a policy is reviewed after implementation may be critical in recognising success and fine tuning aspects of the policy which may not be as effective as they could be. Time spent in review is valuable, but must be accompanied by a willingness to make changes if needed. As a process, review should be constructively critical. Those who have been most closely associated with the writing of a policy will have invested time and hard work in its development. This is an opportunity for all charged with the responsibility of implementation to suggest improvements, but should not be seen as a time for criticising the writers. The policy map, if used as described, should have been the basis for consultation throughout and, by the time a policy reaches implementation, it should have done so on the basis of general consensus.

Activity 4: the review stage

As with the previous stages, there is a sheet (Figure 3.9) to help you with note-making for this stage and, as with the other stages of the process, the six questions should be asked. During this stage you will complete the row marked R (review) on your policy map.

1. Where are we now?

- Has the policy been fully implemented?
- Is everybody implementing it consistently?
- Are all aspects of the policy fully understood?
- Are there any obvious difficulties with the policy?

2. Where do we want to be?

- Which aspects of the policy do we wish to change?
- What could make the policy more effective?
- Is there a need for anyone to change their role in relation to this policy?
- Are there further training needs?

Figure 3.9 Policy review stage activity

POLICY REVIEW STAGE ACTIVITY

Having implemented your policy, you will need to review its effectiveness. Answer these questions before completing the **REVIEW** stage of your policy map.

> What questions will the policy review ask?

> What methods will we take to gather the information?

> What actions will we take following the review?

3. **What must we do?**

■ Will we need to rewrite parts of the policy or is it a matter of applying more consistently that which has already been written?

4. **What is the collective responsibility of people in the school community?**

■ What information is required from people?
■ Who will collate the information and how will it be used?
■ Is there a need for any classroom observation?
■ What information has been gained through monitoring?

5. **What is my responsibility?**

■ What information must I supply?
■ Can I identify further training needs?
■ Do I have a role to play in rewriting?
■ Have I applied the new policy as was intended and agreed?

6. **How long will it take?**

■ Will we review the whole policy or one part of it?
■ How much change is required?

■ How does this review fit in to other aspects of the school's development at this time?

Once the review is completed (see Figure 3.10), it is then possible to use the questions from the planning section to assist in moving forward.

Policy roles and responsibilities

Governors

Within the planning process outlined in this chapter, responsibilities for taking specific actions have been emphasised. The revised *SEN Code of Practice* (DfES 2001a) makes clear that, within schools, specific responsibilities for the management of special educational needs must be firmly established. The duties of the special needs governor and the governing body as a whole, including the overseeing of policies, are clearly articulated in Chapter 1 of the Code. Governors are charged with responsibility for playing a major role in school self-review and the monitoring of the school's special needs policy. In many schools, individual governors are assigned a role in relation to specific subjects or areas of the curriculum. Where this role is effectively fulfilled, governors establish a well-defined working relationship with subject co-ordinators and assist by providing a critical overview of the development and management of the subject throughout the school (for a discussion of subject co-ordination, see Chapter 8).

In order to perform an effective and supportive role in relation to the school curriculum and its development, governors require a well-defined brief. Figure 3.11 provides an example of a brief which might be adopted for governors with a curriculum responsibility.

SENCOs

The role of the special educational needs co-ordinator (SENCO) is clearly established in Chapter 4 of the *SEN Code of Practice* (DfES 2001a). With regards to the curriculum, the support that SENCOs can provide to their colleagues in the development and implementation of policy is critical. While acknowledging that subject co-ordinators are likely to have knowledge and expertise which the SENCO may not have, it is equally likely that the SENCO will need to maintain an overview of all aspects of curriculum planning and documentation in order to ensure accessibility for the whole school population. SENCOs should be consulted with regards to the potential impact of policy changes and development upon pupils with special educational needs. They are likely to have a good knowledge of available resources and equipment to support curriculum access and will need to have an input at each stage of the policy planning process. In many schools, the SENCO is established as a member of the school senior management team and is in a position to influence policy planning. In situations where this is not the case, school managers will need to ensure that the expertise of the SENCO is used effectively to enable policies to become inclusive documents for the benefit of the whole school population.

SENCOs may wish to ask key questions in relation to school curriculum policies and their likely impact upon pupils with special educational needs.

■ Does the policy recognise the needs of all pupils?
■ Are there resource implications in respect of pupils with SEN?

Figure 3.10 Example of a completed policy planning map

POLICY PLANNING MAP

School: Waterside Primary **Policy: Maths**

	Where are we now?	Where do we want to be?	What must we do?	Collective responsibility	My responsibility	Timescale
P	No policy. Identified need to improve consistent teaching approaches.	Clear guidelines for all staff. Information for parents and others. Shared vision.	Form a working group to include governor. Conduct an audit of current practice. Review resources. Establish staff development needs.	Staff to contribute ideas and share current practice. Working party to meet weekly. All staff to read and comment on documents as produced.	To share my ideas. To attend meetings if requested. To catalogue my maths resources. To read and comment on documents at each stage.	Working group established by autumn half-term. Audit to be finished by end of term.
F	Working group established and brief defined.	Policy in place with clear guidelines and agreement of staff.	Working group to meet weekly. Drafts to be circulated to staff for consultation. Final version to go to governors for ratification. Presentation to all staff.	Working group to give commitment to meetings. Each member to share ideas and to consult with all staff. Writing of drafts and final policy.	To consult with specific members of staff. To examine one area of current maths practice (shape and space) and report findings.	Group meeting weekly to produce draft by spring half-term. Final policy by Easter. Ratification by governors at May meeting.
I	Policy available to all staff and ratified by governors.	Policy being referred to consistently by all staff, and influencing practice of maths teaching. Policy understood by parents.	Implementation of policy to be monitored by members of the working group. Workshop session to present policy to parents.	All staff to read and adjust practice to meet the requirements of the policy. Any problems to be brought to attention of working group.	To assist with monitoring. To ensure that my own practice is consistent with the policy.	Policy implemented in September. Workshops for staff and for parents during summer term.
R	Policy in practice and applied by all staff. Staff and parents clear about content and purpose.	Any needs for modification identified through practice to be noted and acted upon.	Questionnaire issued to all staff and analysed by working group. Any modifications needed to be noted and acted upon.	Staff to notify any parts of policy that are problematic. All staff to complete questionnaires.	To help compile, distribute and collect questionnaires. To assist with any rewriting that may be necessary.	Review to be conducted during autumn term after summer implementation. Changes to be made before Christmas.

Figure 3.11 Example of a briefing for governors

Governor Curriculum Duties

Subject: Mathematics

The role of the Governor is to support and work collaboratively with the mathematics co-ordinator, to meet with her on a regular basis and to undertake the following duties.

To become familiar with the approaches to teaching mathematics throughout the school, including the management and implementation of the National Numeracy Strategy.

To become familiar with the resources used for the teaching of mathematics throughout the school.

To meet termly with the mathematics co-ordinator to discuss current development, issues and achievement within the subject.

To attend where possible such training related to the delivery of the mathematics curriculum as may be offered by the school or through the LEA Governors Service.

To keep abreast of national developments and policies related to the teaching of mathematics through reading documentation supplied via the school.

To endeavour to visit classes for the purpose of observing the teaching of mathematics and, related to these observations, to engage in discussion with teachers and other staff regarding the teaching seen.

To support the mathematics co-ordinator as a 'critical friend' and to be available to discuss all aspects of the mathematics curriculum within the school.

To liaise with other governors who have curriculum responsibilities and with the special educational needs co-ordinator (SENCO) in support of the school's policies for curriculum development.

To provide at the request of the Chair of Governors such information as may be required for the annual report to parents.

To report annually to the Board of Governors on developments in mathematics throughout the school.

- Are there training implications for staff who will need to deliver this policy to pupils with SEN?
- Will pupils with SEN need support in being prepared for the implementation of new policy?
- Will there be a need to adjust or modify procedures or paperwork in order to ensure that the policy addresses the needs of all pupils?
- How will the impact of the policy upon pupils with SEN be monitored?

Policies should be used to assist schools in becoming more effective. As such, they should be controlled by the school and should not become the controlling influence of the school. The policy that does not have any influence upon practice is not worth the paper on which it is written. The model provided above should help to ensure that everyone involved with the school feels some ownership of the policy, but that it is developed in a structured, manageable way.

The importance of schools taking responsibility for their own self-review has gained increased currency during the past few years. In recognition of the strides that schools have taken in becoming more reflective with regards to their own development, Ofsted have adopted a lighter touch approach to inspection and have issued advice related to school self-review. It is suggested that the school that understands itself is well on the way to solving any problems it has. Effective school policy development is not only about identifying problems and needs, but should also give some time for acknowledging achievements and successes. As schools have become more efficient in managing the policy development process, they have increased their awareness of those steps that have been taken to increase the participation of all pupils and to support staff in addressing the management of pupils with a wide range of needs. While the initial stages of policy development will inevitably take time, the benefits that accrue from careful management of the process are likely to be a major factor in terms of how all other aspects of the curriculum development of the school are managed.

Long-term planning

Breadth, balance and relevance ...

... in the whole curriculum

Chapter 2 has clarified the statutory position regarding the discretion that schools can now exercise in their whole curriculum planning in order to ensure relevance. While breadth remains an entitlement, we suggest that curricular balance should be managed so as to encompass a flexible range of possibilities, changing from year to year, from pupil to pupil, in order to maintain a focus upon priority needs. Chapter 3 has given a practical means of translating whole curriculum debate into formal policy. Curriculum planning may then be used to control breadth and balance across the whole curriculum and within subjects. Long-term plans should show, for instance, that an appropriate proportion of curriculum time is devoted to the aims and content of the core subjects of the National Curriculum while ensuring the place of other priorities for pupils with learning difficulties within the whole curriculum.

Curriculum maps showing a framework, in outline, of the discrete units or modules to be taught in a given key stage or time frame can provide a useful overview of balance in the curriculum. Continuing aspects of the curriculum may then be taught either in the course of these units, as ongoing concerns integrated with unit content, or in separately timetabled sessions.

Many schools resolve some of the difficulties of timetable planning by rotating certain subjects within their curriculum plans. This sort of approach has certainly found favour with some schools when managing the delivery of foundation subjects. For example, staff may decide that an emphasis will be placed upon teaching an aspect of history to pupils in a given key stage during a particular term, providing coverage in depth in regularly timetabled sessions. In the following term, in order to secure time to focus on another subject, history may not be timetabled in discrete sessions, though opportunities to access or reinforce elements of historical learning within other subjects may be recognised. When schools operate this kind of rotational approach, long-term plans can show that balance is maintained in the whole curriculum over time.

... within subjects

As well as supporting the management of whole curriculum balance, long-term plans should demonstrate that a balanced approach is taken to the teaching of different aspects of a particular subject (for example, that literacy skills are addressed in a given key stage but in an appropriate relationship with drama or communication work). It is the responsibility of subject co-ordinators, in dialogue with curriculum review teams (see Chapter 9) to promote and manage balance within subjects at the long-term planning stage.

Part of this task entails making decisions about aspects of subjects that are to be covered in depth and those that may be treated in outline. As the National Curriculum has been subjected to a series of review processes over the years, one of the consistent purposes has been to reduce prescription and increase flexibility. For example, after the revisions of the 1990s (Dearing 1993a, 1993b), it was claimed that:

> At every key stage, there is far greater freedom within subjects to exemplify broad principles in different ways and to treat some topics in outline and others in depth.
>
> (Tate 1994: 19)

The significance of this discretionary flexibility for teachers working with pupils with special educational needs was emphasised:

> These decisions on depth of coverage of aspects of the programmes of study are key to ensuring that 'freed-up time' remains a reality for teachers of all pupils including those with SEN, and that the elements of the programmes of study which are essential to pupils' progress are taught appropriately.   (Stevens 1995: 31)

More recently, the QCA/DfEE (2001a) *General Guidelines* state that schools should 'meet the needs of their pupils by emphasising particular parts of the curriculum' (p. 12) and that this may entail, among other things:

- devoting 'significant time' to those aspects of the curriculum that constitute 'priorities' for pupils;
- treating 'some parts of a subject in depth' and other material 'with a lighter touch';
- focusing on 'aspects of the programmes of study that are essential for the needs of their pupils';
- emphasising certain skills that require 'regular and frequent practice and teaching'.

> (QCA/DfEE 2001a: 13)

This suggests that staff should feel confident in arriving at informed professional judgements in order to ensure relevance in addition to breadth and balance as they implement the National Curriculum. These decisions will be negotiated and ratified through the sorts of curriculum management processes described in this book and documented in policy statements, curriculum plans, timetables and, where appropriate, individual education plans. There will be no need to follow more formal routes to modification or disapplication unless no attempt is to be made to cover parts of the programmes of study in any form for an entire cohort of pupils.

In addition to managing balance within subjects, staff, as they make their long-term plans, will also begin to document and expand upon the decisions made about aspects of subjects which are to be treated as 'continuing' work or as discrete, 'blocked' units (see Chapter 2). This fundamental distinction will also help staff to manage breadth, balance and relevance. It may, for instance, be important to ensure that aspects of the curriculum that are of crucial significance to pupils are taught continuously and in depth in regular sessions. Other, less essential but nonetheless accessible, interesting, broadening aspects of the curriculum which pupils are entitled to experience, may be taught through a rolling programme of occasional topics or through single stand-alone units or modules (see Chapter 5).

It is important to realise that discussions about how subjects should be taught will not always lead to consistent conclusions. It may, for example, be appropriate to teach part of the mathematics curriculum through a modular approach in one department and through integrated schemes of work in another. Using both approaches, over time, with the same group of pupils may also have a number of advantages. Employing a variety of approaches may mean that the learning needs of a greater number of pupils will be more precisely addressed (Byers 1994a; Babbage *et al.* 1999). It is clear that some pupils learn better in one situation than in another. Providing a balanced mix of teaching methods and learning opportunities will also enable pupils to reinforce their learning by applying it in a range of contexts.

Continuing work

The key skills and other priorities for learning

Although rates of individual progress may be variable, continuity between learning experiences should be seen as an entitlement for all. In many schools, the 'continuing' aspects of the curriculum, and in particular the key skills (see Chapter 2), are used to secure continuity for pupils across the curriculum and through year groups and key stages. This way of working can make it possible, for example, to ensure that:

- communication skills are seen as a priority for many pupils, whether they are in an English lesson, the swimming pool or the dining hall queue, and whether they are chronologically in Key Stage 1 or Key Stage 4;
- encouraging attention control is treated as an important prerequisite for some pupils, whatever the learning context;
- numeracy skills are practised and extended in a range of situations across the curriculum.

When skills like these are highlighted in curriculum plans (as well as in individual education plans where appropriate – see Chapter 7), pupils can be encouraged to work towards important learning outcomes consistently in a range of contexts. They may also be enabled to pursue developmentally appropriate goals even as the age-related content of lessons builds.

It may be helpful to indicate this function of the key skills within long-term plans by summarising the range of typical possibilities under each of the skill headings. The *Developing Skills* booklet from QCA/DfES (2001b) takes this process forward and provides a useful starting point for further development work in schools. Figure 4.1 shows a statement about cross-curricular skills used in one all-age school for pupils with severe learning difficulties. It should be noted that this is neither a checklist nor an exhaustive audit of all the cross-curricular work undertaken by the school's pupils. It is, however, a useful statement reminding staff that all schemes of work have the potential for allowing pupils to pursue relevant, individual, cross-curricular targets (see Chapter 7).

Continuing skills and processes in the subjects

It is also possible to identify work that should be treated on a continuing basis in the programmes of study for specific subjects (see Chapter 2). As SCAA (1995) notes, 'skills acquired in one subject or aspect of the curriculum can be applied or consolidated in another'.

In Figure 4.2, staff at the same school for pupils with severe learning difficulties have set aside the continuing aspects, as they see them, of the programmes of study for science, geography and history at Key Stage 1. As we shall see later in this chapter,

---

Figure 4.1 Example of a statement about cross-curricular skills

Cross-curricular Skills and Schemes of Work

All activities will provide contexts in which pupils can apply, practise and develop transferable, cross-curricular skills. The range of skills will encompass:

- **communication skills** – from eye contact and interaction through the use of gesture, signs and symbols to speaking, listening, reading and writing

- **numeracy skills** – from matching, sorting, grouping and sequencing through predicting, estimating, comparing and classifying to practical skills involving money, time and measurement

- **study skills** – from attending, concentrating, and being willing to focus on task through skills in selecting and organising an environment or position in which to work to researching, managing time and collating information

- **problem-solving skills** – from an awareness of cause and effect through choice and decision-making to investigative activities in which pupils learn from their experiences collaboratively

- **personal and social skills** – from basic personal hygiene, feeding and dressing skills through to health education, home economics and self-organisation programmes

- **information technology skills** – from the control of single switches, touch screens and concept keyboards through to word processing, data handling and keyboard skills

- **perceptual skills** – from the perception of colour, pattern, shape, position, relationship and equivalence through to the making of fine judgements and measurements

- **physical skills** – from skills of positioning and mobility through to fine and gross motor skills and hand-eye co-ordination.

---

the schemes of work relating to rolling programmes of units can acknowledge these kinds of links between subjects. In this statement, an effort has been made to interpret and extend the language of the programmes of study in order to emphasise relevance and continuity with the school's particular curricular concerns. Although the schemes of work themselves acknowledge content from the later key stages, the statement about continuing skills and processes relates essentially to the programmes of study for Key Stage 1. This is because the school considers it probable that many pupils will continue to develop skills, knowledge and understanding at the earliest levels even as they engage with age-appropriate subject content as they grow older. In other circumstances, continuing work from the programmes of study for later key stages could be represented in such a statement or in separate statements prepared for different age groupings of pupils.

Much of the science represented here concerns experimental and investigative methods, which are acknowledged as having cross-curricular significance. There are also skills and processes with which pupils will engage whenever they are involved in historical enquiry or geographical investigation. Presenting the continuing aspects of particular programmes of study as statements within long-term plans will also work for other subjects – for the general requirements for physical education, art or music, for instance. In many senses, this way of approaching the continuing aspects of the subjects will contribute significantly to the debate, and to policy-making, about

Figure 4.2 Example of a statement about continuing skills and processes

Continuing Skills and Processes

All schemes of work in science, geography and history will provide contexts in which pupils will be encouraged to:

- use all their available senses to observe and explore at first hand

- communicate awareness and understanding orally, visually, through role play, information technology and in writing

- build scientific, geographical and historical vocabularies in words, gestures, signs or symbols

- develop skills in sorting, grouping, comparing, classifying, sequencing and measuring

- identify and describe similarities and differences

- learn from stories, descriptions, eyewitness reports, demonstrations, books, pictures, videos, tapes, television and information technology in addition to first-hand experience

- participate in processes involving investigation, exploration, enquiry, problem-solving and group activity

- use visits, fieldwork, practical activities, direct experience and everyday situations as starting points for enquiry

- use sources, experiences and their own ideas in order to make discoveries, ask questions, promote ideas, test hypotheses and draw conclusions

- obtain, respond to, select, store and retrieve information

- report and interpret findings and data

- record and present findings in a variety of ways, including pictures, diagrams, models, charts, actions, songs, speech, writing, signs, symbols, tapes, video and information technology

- identify different ways of presenting ideas

- relate ideas to evidence, finding connections and causal relationships between events

- test predictions against evidence and generate explanations

- recognise when tests or comparisons are unfair and when conclusions are not supported by evidence

- acquire knowledge, skills and understanding and relate their learning to everyday life and personal experience

- follow instructions and directions and plan work independently

- recognise and control hazards and risks

- become aware of the passage of time and of the world beyond their own locality

- consider how to treat living things and the environment with care and sensitivity.

teaching approaches and learning styles and effective ways of promoting learning for pupils with special educational needs. Schools may wish to develop some of the ideas they identify as continuing aspects of subjects in more general 'access statements' about effective teaching approaches and learning styles.

However, these statements will not constitute detailed schemes of work from which staff can plan group sessions or individual objectives. Schools may wish to increase levels of detail for some subjects. Staff may produce extended programmes of study for the use and application of mathematics, or speaking and listening in English, constituting medium-term plans (see Chapter 5) reflecting work undertaken in regular timetable slots. Similarly, the development of information technology capability may merit detailed planning at the medium-term level. It may require space on the timetable as a subject-specific lesson in Key Stages 3 and 4 while being delivered continuously across the curriculum in Key Stages 1 and 2. Schools may wish to experiment with statements about continuing skills and processes while constructing long-term plans for a range of subjects.

Discrete units of work

Where the continuing aspects of subjects are set aside in long-term plans as discussed above, a task remains to deal with that material which can be treated as a series of discrete units of work. These discrete units may be developed as recurring cycles of work, with pupils returning regularly to concepts presented in revised, age-appropriate contexts several times through a key stage or school career. This model works particularly well for younger pupils in relation to the programmes of study for Key Stages 1 and 2. Many senior schools opt to present a series of stand-alone modules of work so that pupils may only come across certain ideas once in the course of Key Stages 3 and 4. This chapter will examine both these strategies and the notion of links between units of work.

Inter-subject links and linked units of work

The process of establishing links between different but related aspects of subjects is not to be confused with strategies relating to the cross-curricular elements – aspects of the curriculum which may be said to permeate a wide range of teaching contexts regardless of subject content – nor the traditional 'topic' in which a single theme was seen as a means of delivering aspects of many subjects. Traditional topic work has been subjected to consistent criticism over the years (some of it summarised in Byers 1992) but more recently the concept of the 'subject-focused topic' or integrated scheme of work has gained credence.

Alexander, Rose and Woodhead (1992) put forward the case for a balance between 'subject and carefully focused topic work' in their report on *Curriculum Organisation and Classroom Practice in Primary Schools*. Ofsted, in their follow-up report (1993), argued that successful topics have 'a single subject bias or emphasise particular subjects'. The National Curriculum Council (1993) described 'well-planned topic work' as being 'focused on a limited range of specific aspects' of the subjects but noted that 'curriculum coherence can be strengthened by linking together, where appropriate, units from different subjects'. Having received official blessing from Sir Ron Dearing in his interim report (1993a), this way of thinking went on to influence SCAA (1995) in the preparation of *Planning the Curriculum at Key Stages 1 and 2*.

This document makes it clear that linking units of work can be productive both because of 'common or complementary knowledge, understanding and skills' and because work in one area can provide 'a useful stimulus for work in another'. The document, like its predecessors, however, warns staff to:

- keep work focused by restricting the number of subjects or aspects of the curriculum to be linked;
- avoid contrived or artificial links between subjects or other aspects of the curriculum.

(SCAA 1995: 44)

and to ensure that any linking does not disrupt progression, balance or the separate integrity of individual subjects.

In summary, traditional whole-school, whole-curriculum 'topics' tend to create problems for staff in managing the content of separate aspects of the curriculum and in recognising and making focused judgements about pupils' achievements in relation to subjects. Pupils may be overwhelmed by poorly related ideas and experience confusion, superficiality and repetition. Making well-judged and limited numbers of links between units of work can be very productive, however. Establishing sound inter-subject links can mean that learning opportunities become seamless, holistic, coherent experiences for pupils while teachers maintain a clear, unambiguous view of strands relating to specific subjects. Schools should make their own decisions about when this is appropriate but be sure that links are carefully planned and constructive and that the progress pupils make in relation to subject-specific knowledge, skills and understanding can be traced through linked units.

Making long-term plans

A plan for Key Stage 1

It is now possible to look at several of these principles in action by looking in detail at examples of the long-term planning process in action. Figure 4.3 represents part of a long-term plan for delivering the curriculum in Key Stage 1 in a school for pupils with severe and profound and multiple learning difficulties. The plan is divided into two years, Year A and Year B, to cover the two years that five- to seven-year-old pupils will spend in Key Stage 1. Year B follows Year A, then the material in Year A is addressed again for a new cohort of pupils coming into Key Stage 1. Each of the years in the rolling programme is divided into three terms, autumn, spring and summer, and, for some subjects, into half-term units. Up to 12 units of work can therefore be delivered across two years in this programme without repetition.

In this school, there is no intention to teach the curriculum in discrete or blocked units of work in all the subjects, however. In Key Stage 1, the programmes of study for English and mathematics, including work relating to the national strategies for literacy and numeracy, will be addressed solely through continuing work, entailing regular daily sessions devoted to English and mathematics. The school notes that there will be other opportunities to teach, practise, consolidate and generalise learning in English and mathematics in a number of contexts across the curriculum in Key Stage 1.

The plan for science involves both continuing work, including regular opportunities for pupils to learn through first-hand sensory experience, and a series of discrete units of work, focused on science, each of which will occupy a term's worth of science lessons. The plan reveals that the school has decided that work on the three content-driven attainment targets will be undertaken in both years of the cycle. Attainment target 2, 'life processes and living things', will be covered in the spring term of both

Figure 4.3 Long-term plan for Key Stage 1

	Year A			Year B		
	Autumn	**Spring**	**Summer**	**Autumn**	**Spring**	**Summer**
English	Ongoing work, both permeating the whole curriculum, the whole day and delivered in regular sessions including the daily literacy hour. These will address speaking and listening and communication skills, including gesture and signing, stories, listening, talking, role playing, reading, writing using symbols.					
Maths	Ongoing work, with key numeracy skills including mathematical language permeating a range of contexts across the curriculum. Daily opportunities for using and applying mathematics in all the areas of number, shape, space and problem-solving in the numeracy lesson each day.					
Science	Ongoing work promoting the skills of first-hand sensory experience, the development of a scientific vocabulary and health and safety issues across the curriculum. A cycle of blocked units promoting experimentation, experiencing and investigation into:					
	Materials – grouping	Life Processes & the Living World: Humans & Plants	Forces & Motion	Materials – changing	Life Processes & the Living World: Plants & Animals	Electricity, Light & Sound
Geography	Continuing work on weather					
	Our school	People who help us	Where I live	Home and away	Pets and Animals	Where I live
History	Personal History	Personal Toys	Personal History	Personal Environment	Time I	Time II
Design & technology	Ongoing work in designing and making, giving opportunities to develop experiences, knowledge and understanding, delivered through regular timetable sessions in art, craft and food technology (cooking).					
	Melt & Freeze	Textiles	Construction	Cakes	Textiles	Construction
Art	Ongoing work promoting practical art and craft skills and developing an appreciation of art across the curriculum. Weekly sessions providing regular opportunities for investigating, experiencing and handling and creating through a wide variety of materials and techniques.					
	Pattern & Texture Collage	Colour – Painting	Line & Tone: Printing	Shape & Form Clay	Line & Tone: Observational Drawing	Colour Primary & Secondary
Music	Ongoing work, with the use of song, rhythm, sound and music contributing to teaching across the curriculum. Regular sessions to provide opportunities for listening and appraising and performing and composing. Specific links with the following blocked units:					
	Explore & experience different sounds	Introduce named classroom instruments	Integrated arts experiences – stop & start	Dynamics loud/quiet/silence	Tempo fast/slow	Pitch high/low
PSHE	Ongoing work promoting consideration of others, taking responsibility for yourself, asking for help, making real choices and promoting a positive self-image to aid independence skills.					
	Body parts and function	Dressing and self-care skills	Dining skills and food	Self-advocacy and relationships	Feelings and emotions	Community and keeping safe

years. Attainment target 3, 'materials and their properties', is also covered in both years with related units on 'materials'. Attainment target 4, 'physical processes', is allocated two units in the cycle, but the school has decided to bring together the work on 'electricity' and 'light and sound' in one unit, reflecting the kinds of decisions about work taught 'in depth' or with a 'lighter touch' that QCA/DfEE (2001a) advocate.

Plans for teaching history and geography are different again. In these subjects, the plan given in Figure 4.3 shows that the school intends to teach these subjects entirely through discrete units of work, apart from offering the pupils regular and ongoing opportunities to observe and record the weather. The history and geography units occupy alternating half-term slots on the timetable. This means that there will not necessarily be a geography and history lesson on the timetable in each week of the year. The school has confidence, however, that the long-term plan shows breadth and balance of coverage of the programmes of study over time and is entirely comfortable with this situation.

Although Figure 4.3 does not show plans for all the subjects in the curriculum, other subjects are dealt with in this long-term plan using a mixture of continuing work and discrete units of work. Each of these aspects of teaching with be planned in more detail through the school's medium-term and short-term planning procedures, but the long-term plan has the merit of providing, on one proforma, an outline of the work to be covered in one key stage. This sheet may, in itself, be a useful record of planned experience to share with learning support staff and parents.

Opportunities to make links between subjects (see above) can also be indicated at this level of planning. Notes are made on the plan in Figure 4.3 about opportunities for 'integrated arts experiences'. Individual teachers will also be able to make their own decisions about the productive relationships that could exist in the classroom, for example, between the grouping of materials in science and collage-making in art in the autumn term of Year A; between changing materials in science and cooking cakes for design and technology in the autumn term of Year B; or between work on plants in science and observational drawing in art in the spring term of Year B. Enabling pupils to explore these kinds of productive links will help to enhance the coherence of the curriculum; the long-term plan will allow staff to maintain the integrity of the content of each subject in their planning and recording.

A plan for Key Stage 3

The school staff who produced the plan given in Figure 4.3 have produced similar plans for the curriculum in the other age groups. There is another two-year cycle for Key Stage 4; a four-year cycle for Key Stage 2, in which some core elements are emphasised a number of times; and a three-year cycle for Key Stage 3. Part of this plan is given here as Figure 4.4. It is interesting to note, in contrast with Figure 4.3, that the school intends to make more use of teaching in discrete units for these 11- to 14-year-old pupils. The English and mathematics schemes of work, while still making use of some elements of continuing work, are divided into termly units addressing aspects of curriculum content that it is appropriate to teach to pupils, including those with learning difficulties, in Key Stage 3. In this way, many of the requirements of the programmes of study for the National Curriculum are met (for example, studying a Shakespeare play and works of fiction by Charles Dickens and Mary Shelley, two major writers published before 1914) but are not adhered to slavishly. We may assume that these pupils, in their work in Key Stage 3 on shape and space, will continue to be taught to 'observe, handle and describe common 2-D and 3-D shapes' (programmes of study for Key Stage 1); 'to classify shapes and solve problems' or 'to visualise 3-D shapes from 2-D drawings' (programmes of study for Key Stage 2); but that they

Figure 4.4 Long-term plan for Key Stage 3

	YEAR 7			YEAR 8			YEAR 9		
	Autumn	Spring	Summer	Autumn	Spring	Summer	Autumn	Spring	Summer
English	Oliver Twist	Romeo & Juliet (Shakespeare)	The media	Adrian Mole	Treasure Island	Poetry/nature	Frankenstein	Lord of the Flies	Travel/letter writing
	Ongoing work – communication – speaking/listening – development of language skills – writing – reading								
Maths	Pattern	Hand data	Shape Space	Measure	Problem-solve	Pattern	Hand data	Shape Space	Measure
	Ongoing maths work – number/time/money								
Science	Forces and motion	Life processes	Human Development	Light and Sound	The Earth	Electricity and Magnetism	Environmental Studies	Classifying materials	Changing materials
½ term History	Britain 1750–1900 (I)	Twentieth-Century World	Britain 1750–1900 (II)	Twentieth-Century World	Ancient America/Australia	Parliament and People 1500–1750	Parliament and People 1500–1750	Era Pre-1914	Medieval realms 1066–1500
½ term Geography	Places – Europe	Weather & Climate	Ecosystems	Places – Europe	Earthquakes & volcanoes	Rivers & floods	Places – Africa	Population & settlement	Economic activities
Physical education	Gymnastics	Games	Athletics	Games	Gymnasium	Athletics	Games	Athletics	Gymnasium
	Activity Room and Swimming – ongoing activity								
Design & technology (School scheme)	Food Sandwich activities	Textiles (Magnet Theatre) Theatre project	Construction Mechanisms investigation	Food Pasta	Textiles Fashion (Tee shirt)	Construction Energy project	Food Fruit & vegetables	Textiles Furnishing project (repeat patterns)	Construction Materials project

might not learn to 'understand, recall and use Pythagoras' theorem' (programmes of study for Key Stage 3). Further discussion of the issue of progression is provided in Chapter 5. Figure 4.5 shows how another school developed a way of managing the complex interactions between age, key stage and skill development in the curriculum for mathematics. Making use of this cumulative mix of material from across the key stages as pupils grow older is entirely appropriate and similar strategies will apply in relation to the curriculum for science in Key Stage 3.

Looking at the units of work set out for study in history and geography lessons in Figure 4.4, however, reveals a close adherence to the breadth of content recommended in the programmes of study for Key Stage 3. These discrete units, drawing on the geographical and historical knowledge, skills and understanding developed in previous key stages, will provide access for teenage pupils to areas of learning that will help them to contextualise themselves as citizens in a modern world and will enable them to engage, relatively briefly, in half-termly units, with an interesting and stimulating range of new experiences. The school's complete long-term plan for Key Stage 3, of course, includes all the subjects of the curriculum that are required to be taught in this age group (including a modern foreign language, swimming, sex education, PSHE, careers and citizenship education). In addition, aspects of continuing teaching and learning that the school considers important for pupils with learning difficulties in their teenage years (road safety, personal hygiene, balanced nutrition, dressing and undressing) are also set out in the long-term plan and implemented. Teaching a broad and balanced curriculum that takes full account of the requirements of the National Curriculum need not force schools to abandon the teaching of those elements that are deemed to be directly relevant to the day-to-day lives of young people with special educational needs in and beyond the classroom. Many schools also build into their long-term plans free spaces in which teachers and pupils can pursue ideas and interests of local or contemporary relevance; revisit work that, by agreement, deserves more attention; or revise areas of learning that become particularly important or that proved problematic the first time they were taught. Staff will appreciate these opportunities to exercise their own professional judgements, often and appropriately in consultation with pupils and parents.

Closing comments

This chapter has explored the key issues of breadth and balance across and within subjects; delineated the useful and constructive distinctions between continuing work and material that can be effectively taught in discrete units of work; and made comments about the potential for making links between subjects. Schools will wish to develop their own processes and formats to support long-term planning. In the next chapter, we discuss options for the medium-term level of planning. We explore ways of ensuring and monitoring progression through strands of study within units of work and address the issue of maintaining the integrity of individual subjects by planning for subject-specific assessment opportunities.

Figure 4.5 Continuing work in mathematics: shape, space and measures – 3-D shapes

	KEY STAGE 1	KEY STAGE 2	KEY STAGE 3	KEY STAGE 4
Handling shapes	Making shapes from Playdoh. Free play with shapes.	Making shapes from clay. Finding shapes in the environment.	Making 3-D shapes in cooking. Bread, biscuits.	Finding 3-D shapes in packaging. Supermarket.
Playing with shapes	Playing with balls. Feely bag of assorted shapes.	Threading beads of different shapes following a pattern.	Finding out if shapes will roll, slide etc.	Making bigger squares from smaller ones. Computer work.
Fitting shapes together	Duplo. Free junk modelling.	Lego. More directed junk modelling, e.g. making a house.	Building with Poleidoblocks, Sticklebricks etc.	Looking at patterns in the environment to show fitting shapes, e.g. bricks, logs, pipes.
Making shapes	Make pictures with 3-D shapes. Regular (e.g. toilet rolls) and irregular (pasta etc.).	Making shapes using templates, e.g. Pyramids connect with Egyptians. Bubbles and cylinders etc.	Papier mâché – using balloons, saucers etc.	Making shapes from nets – link with programme for 2-D shapes.
Matching shapes	Matching boards. Matching like to like.	Using paint to print faces – match back to 3-D shape.	Finding shapes in the environment by planning a shape trail.	Finding shapes in the home.
Sorting shapes	Sort informally according to shape. Tidying away.	Sort according to set criteria, triangles, cuboids, squares. Putting shapes back in boxes.	Sort according to attributes. How may corners, sides etc.	Sorting using tree diagrams. Using two or more attributes.
Matching and sorting named shapes	Simple games. Can you find a...?	Matching words/symbols to shapes. Putting into labelled boxes.	Putting away cutlery, crockery etc. in the practical room.	Finding containers for a purpose, e.g. a box to put pencils in from a variety of different shapes.
Recognising named 3-D shapes	Playing games to help recognition of simple 3-D shapes.	Using Language Master cards to match word to shape.	Labelling groceries according to shape, word or symbol.	Computer programs matching word with shape.
Generalising naming/ signing shapes	Can inform another child the name of the basic shape. Speaking or signing.	Can label shapes in the classroom using words or symbols.	Following instructions on Language Master or tape. Find three cylinders etc.	Making shapes with straws following instructions.
Finding properties of shapes	Finding a shape when given name, when blindfolded and describing it.	Finding a shape when blindfolded from a description.	Sorting by attributes of properties. Can stack, can fit together etc.	Combining shapes to make new shapes. Relabelling.

5 Medium-term planning

In practical terms, there may be overlap between long-term, medium-term and short-term plans. In many schools, the kind of planning we describe in this chapter is seen as part of long-term documentation – or, indeed, in other cases as an aspect of short-term development. This is entirely appropriate. As we indicated in Chapter 1, there is no set formula for the preparation of schemes of work and it is for individual schools to interpret the categories of planning we offer in the light of their own needs and priorities and to adapt the ideas we put forward for their own use.

What is clear, however, is that there is a task which lies between the stage of planning we described in Chapter 4 – where broad aims and intentions with regard to content, coverage, continuity and links between subjects are set out over a timescale measured in key stages and year groups – and the processes we will elaborate in Chapter 6 which are concerned with ensuring that individual pupils, in particular classes, have meaningful learning experiences day to day and week by week.

In accordance with National Curriculum terminology (SCAA 1995, 1996; QCA/DfEE 2001a), we refer to this intermediate stage in the planning process as medium-term. In many senses, however, the developments we detail in this chapter comprise the next logical steps in refining those formal documents which we have referred to as long-term plans. There is no necessity to view the work we describe in this chapter as a separate part of what should be, in our view, a seamless process.

In Chapter 4 we discussed the notion of curricular continuity in some detail. We now wish to turn to the parallel concept of progression.

Progression

Progression as differentiation

If the key skills and cross-curricular processes that we identified as 'continuing' work lend coherence and continuity to the curriculum, it is the structured sequencing of experiences that can ensure that the curriculum offers meaningful progression for pupils. A sense of progression through the continuing aspects of the curriculum has already been built into the process statements which we discussed in Chapter 4. Planning for progress and achievement for individual pupils will be described in Chapter 6. This chapter will explore progression as a dimension in curriculum planning and the sequencing of experiences and opportunities within discrete units of work. Medium-term planning will, in this way, help to secure progress towards subject-related objectives and age-appropriate experiences for notional groups of pupils at different age stages.

All pupils have a right to expect that learning experiences will be presented in a coherent sequence. Clearly, individual pupils will progress at different rates according to their interests, previous achievements and aptitudes for particular subjects (see Chapters 6 and 7). However, medium-term plans for discrete units of work can be used to generate a framework which typifies and exemplifies progression for representative groups of pupils at various stages in their school careers.

Four kinds of progression

The QCA/DfEE (2001a) *General Guidelines* to support *Planning, Teaching and Assessing the Curriculum for Pupils with Learning Difficulties* set out eight 'different forms of progression' that can be highlighted in planning. These include progression in terms of:

- engagement in negotiated learning, where pupils are encouraged to take a greater part in the learning process and in planning or measuring success;
- response to a range of teaching methods, determined by pupils' different strengths and learning preferences at different stages of development;
- use of a variety of support equipment to enable pupils to take control of their environment; to increase mobility; to develop and practise communication skills.

(p. 15)

While we endorse these exhaustive ways of conceptualising and managing progression, we suggest that staff may find it helpful to think about planning for progression in four broad areas:

- **skill development**
  gaining new skills and/or maintaining, refining, combining, consolidating, transferring and generalising existing skills;
- **entitlement to content**
  extending access to knowledge and understanding into new areas as pupils grow older;
- **learning contexts**
  ensuring that activities, resources, environments, approaches and attitudes are appropriate to pupils' ages and interests;
- **functional application**
  moving away from adult dependence and classroom-based activity towards independence and practical, community-orientated activity.

Although presenting and discussing these categories separately may help to clarify thinking, they are clearly interrelated. Planning and practice should ensure that these different forms of progression support one another in ways that are constructive for pupils with learning difficulties.

Skill development

Progression in terms of skill development will be a familiar concept to anyone who has a background in working with pupils with learning difficulties. For many years the curriculum for these pupils was founded upon checklists of developmentally sequenced hierarchies of such skills. While the teaching of skills in isolation is unlikely to be helpful for a pupil in terms of generalising learning, there is certainly a case to be made for anticipating the development of those skills that will enable a pupil to make smooth progress through a lesson or series of lessons. Indeed, the National Curriculum proposes that it is important for pupils to gain skills related to specific subjects, often as a preparation for meaningful participation in more complex, investigative activity (Sebba *et al.* 1993). In this book we have also examined the notion of key, cross-curricular skills which may be developed in a range of contexts across the curriculum (Chapter 4). We have noted that it is possible for pupils to progress in terms of their communication skills whether they are in an English lesson, conducting a science experiment or riding a horse. Clearly, it is also important to expect and plan for progress in relation to subject-specific skills, whether these are seen as part of the continuing work in a subject (see Chapter 4) or as an objective within a discrete unit. There is clear progression in the programmes of study for music, for example, between describing sounds 'using given and invented signs and symbols' (Key Stage 1) and being taught to use 'staff notation' (Key Stage 3). This development of the skill of recording would be represented in units of work designed to give pupils opportunities to apply their musical knowledge and understanding.

We would also encourage staff to note that progression may not always mean that *new* skills are being developed. For some pupils, using an existing skill spontaneously or consistently, more confidently or more fluently, in an unfamiliar situation or with new people may constitute very significant progress. Similarly, for other pupils, simply continuing to use a skill, or reactivating a previously established skill after a lapse in use, may be important evidence that regression is not taking place or, at least, is not accelerating. Again, these achievements should be considered, and acknowledged in curriculum planning, as forms of skill development.

Entitlement to new content

Even where pupils' achievements in terms of skill development remain focused on small increments of progress at the earliest levels, there is an entitlement to learn about new ideas as they grow older. In science, for instance, pupils in Key Stage 1 should be taught simply that 'humans and other animals can produce offspring and that these offspring grow into adults.' By the time these pupils are teenagers, with a legal entitlement to information and teaching about their sexuality (Scott 1994), they should know, according to the National Curriculum, about 'the physical and emotional changes that take place during adolescence'; about 'the menstrual cycle and fertilisation'; and about 'the human reproductive system' and foetal development. A comprehensive programme of personal and social education would probably also suggest that they should learn, among other things, about relationships, parenting and the right to choice and self-determination in sexual behaviour in addition to knowing the stark facts of human reproduction (McLaughlin and Byers 2001).

Of course, creating access to this kind of awareness for pupils who, in terms of their skills and other areas of understanding, are still working on material based in the programmes of study for Key Stage 1 is a challenge. But it is a challenge that an entitlement curriculum requires us to meet. Units of work devised for older pupils will need to show routes of access to breadth of content which becomes an entitlement as a facet of progression.

Age-appropriate contexts

Thirdly, pupils have a right to expect that their learning, as they mature, will take place in age-appropriate contexts. Pupils may still need practice in learning how to 'recognise and use simple spelling patterns' (programmes of study for English, Key Stage 1) when they are 14. They should probably not, however, be exercising these competencies in writing a story about Flopsy-Wopsy Bunny and the Cuddly Kangaroo. The programmes of study for English at Key Stages 3 and 4 give a wide range of forms of writing which are both age-appropriate ('diaries ... information leaflets ... letters conveying opinions ... reviews ... reports ...') and accessible at early levels of skill development, particularly in view of the statutory position on adaptations to modes of access (see Chapter 1).

The notion of being age-appropriate should not become a dogma that leads to demeaning tokenism or stands in the way of work that is genuinely enjoyed by, and developmentally appropriate for, individual pupils. Nind and Hewett (1994) make a compelling case for continuing to provide intensive interaction, without regard to chronological age, for pupils who experience profound difficulties in communication. It makes no sense to deprive a pupil of a favourite programme of recorded music simply because it appears 'childish'. There is no rule that dictates that all teenagers will listen to the latest chart-topping pop combo or, indeed, be dressed in the same adult interpretation of what constitutes young persons' fashion.

However, there is also a strong case to be made for designing schemes of work that broaden pupils' horizons in a number of ways – in terms, for example, of age-appropriate teaching methods; learning that is increasingly co-operative and negotiated in style; and support that is gradually but steadily withdrawn. Planning that is age-appropriate should offer pupils access to an ever-increasing range of options and experiences as they grow older. This may be especially true for pupils with learning difficulties who may not have other opportunities to engage with the culture of adolescence; who may be sheltered and protected from the world beyond home and school; and who may find emancipation from parents and childhood difficult to achieve (Griffiths 1994).

Progress towards functional application

Emphasising the practical, functional application of skills learned in school is not simply part of the process of locating work in age-appropriate contexts. Encouraging pupils to put the skills they have learned in the classroom to use in the community entails more than a change of place. It also involves pupils in shedding their dependence upon staff support and adult consensus and engaging in independent, self-motivated activity. Learning to 'follow safe procedures' (programmes of study for design and technology, Key Stage 1) may be a reasonable expectation of a pupil making a sandwich in the school kitchen. Offering that same pupil a work experience placement making up fencing panels in a timber yard may involve risk-taking of a totally different order, although this is presumably precisely where units of work in design and technology might be seen to lead for some pupils. Again, counting coins in class in order to 'explore and record ... patterns of multiples of 2, 5 and 10' (programmes of study for mathematics, Key Stage 1) will not fully prepare pupils for the complex demands of paying for goods at the supermarket checkout and counting the change. Well-planned units of work can bring the practical application of school-based competencies into focus for staff and pupils alike and guide pupils progressively towards the goal of independence in the community.

Planning for progression in units of work

Returning to the long-term plans for units of work we examined in Chapter 4, it will be possible to see some of these principles in action as detail exemplifying strands of progression is built into medium-term plans. Let us consider the strands of content, drawing on the programmes of study for science and geography in the National Curriculum, concerned with 'Plants, Animals, Weather and Climate' in the long-term plans for the curriculum in an all-age school for pupils with severe learning difficulties.

The curriculum development team in this school now need to design separate but related responses to teaching these aspects of content to pupils in each of four distinct age stages (Figure 5.1).

The challenge is to pursue the strands (set in bold type) identified for this unit of work at the long-term planning stage through each of the age stages (2–7, 7–11, 11–14, 14–19). Classroom activity, characteristic of each age stage and showing progression, is exemplified in italics. While all of the work represented in this unit may be said to be founded in the Key Stage 1 programmes of study for science and geography (see Chapter 4), the activities in each age stage build sequentially upon previous learning and introduce new skills, content, contexts and applications.

The strand dealing with 'weather and climate' shows clear progress in terms of skill development (Figure 5.1). While the youngest pupils use pictures of the weather to decide if it is cloudy or sunny today, the 7–11-year-olds use symbols to make bar charts as weather records. The pupils in the 11–14 age stage move on to work with standard meteorological symbols and national weather maps while the oldest pupils note patterns in the weather forecasts in the media.

An entitlement to new content is reflected in this unit by the widening focus which takes pupils from a study of today's weather, outside the classroom window, in the early years towards an understanding of different climates around the world and their impact upon environmental issues globally (Figure 5.1, 'Climatic effects'). Pupils could be said to have a right to understand about local water conservation measures as well as some of the origins of drought in the developing countries of the world – both issues which they are likely to encounter in the course of watching television.

It should be stressed here that this matrix of exemplified activity does not require pupils to consolidate all the learning from one age stage before moving on to the next. As with the National Curriculum model, there is flexibility between stages and a notion that the work in the unit is cumulative. Thus it will be possible for pupils to continue to identify and name parts of animals (Figure 5.1, 'Life cycles', age 2–7) when they are 13, but they might then be encouraged to work on these concepts in the context of age-appropriate experiences relating to animals at work (Figure 5.1, 'Life cycles', age 14–19).

If this unit provides age-appropriate contexts for developmentally appropriate activity, it also encourages progress towards functional application. The strand concerned with 'Care, welfare and needs' (Figure 5.1) provides the youngest pupils with opportunities to identify the difference between plants and animals that are alive and items that are 'not alive'. In later years, other sessions will contribute to pupils' understandings about animals' food needs and about reproduction, giving access to aspects of the programmes of study for science in Key Stages 2 and 3 ('Life processes' including 'Nutrition'). By the time pupils are 16, however, they may be learning to take independent responsibility for the care of animals as part of a work experience programme, thus integrating aspects of scientific and geographical study with their careers education and applying the skills they have learned in school to 'real world' situations.

It will be noted that activities relating to citizenship and aspects of the school curriculum such as work-related learning and education for sustainable development become increasingly important for the older pupils in other strands of this unit. In fact, they lend a characteristic flavour of preparation for the world of work and adult life to the work planned for students in the 14–19 curriculum.

If schools wish to explore the notion of planning for progression by exemplifying activity, they may draw up blank versions of the format given in Figure 5.1. These can then be used and adapted for planning and auditing or monitoring purposes. The

Figure 5.1a Strands of progression in Unit 2

Unit 2 – Plants, Animals, Weather and Climate

2–7	7–11	11–14	14–19
Variety of life Identifying and naming ■ domestic pets e.g. cat, dog, fish, rabbit ■ farm animals e.g. cow, sheep, chicken, pig ■ garden dwellers and mini-beasts e.g. trees, flowers, worms, butterflies, ladybirds	**Variety of life** Identifying and naming ■ zoo animals e.g. lion, bear, giraffe, elephant ■ wild animals e.g. fox, mouse, pigeon, seagull ■ local habitats and environments e.g. woods, beaches, fields, rivers	**Variety of life** Identifying, classifying and grouping by categories ■ of creatures e.g. fish, birds, insects, mammals, reptiles, amphibians ■ of vegetation e.g. cactus/desert, tree/forest, grass/savanna ■ of plants and animals in their habitats e.g. birds/hedges, fish/sea	**Variety of life** Evolution and extinction e.g. origins of humanity, fossils, endangered species, dinosaurs Ecology and conservation e.g. rainforest, ponds, woodland, hedgerows habitat destruction, pollution, resource management Plants and animals in their habitats e.g. waders/estuaries, frogs/ponds, dolphins/oceans
Life cycles Identifying and naming parts ■ of animals e.g. head, leg, ears, eyes, tail ■ of plants e.g. leaf, flower	**Life cycles** Identifying and naming parts and characteristics ■ of animals e.g. wings, beak, claws, paws, fins, ■ of plants e.g. roots, stems, petals, seeds	**Life cycles** Reproduction, birth and death, life cycles ■ of animals, e.g. eggs/chicks, spawn/frogs, caterpillar/butterfly, young/adult ■ of plants e.g. germination, growth, flowering, seeds, pollination	**Life cycles** Animals at work e.g. police dogs, carrier pigeons, horses Animals for food and profit e.g. poultry, eggs, milk, cheese, wool, bacon, meat Exploitation of plant life e.g. timber, paper, arable farming
Care, welfare and needs Alive and not alive e.g. animals and plants v. rocks and toys Respect for living things e.g. not hurting, not damaging	**Care, welfare and needs** Movement, feeding, use of senses ■ in animals e.g. food, water, warmth, shelter, exercise, response to sound/smell ■ in plants e.g. growing seeds, planting bulbs, water, response to light	**Care, welfare and needs** Growth and reproduction ■ of animals e.g. food chain, feeding young, milk, nests, burrows ■ of plants e.g. gardening, water cycle, fertilisers, soil enrichment, root feeding	**Care, welfare and needs** Independent responsibility ■ for animals e.g. feeding/grooming/walking the dog, stable/farm work experience ■ for plants e.g. house plants/window boxes/flower beds, horticultural work experience

Figure 5.1b Strands of progression in Unit 2 (continued)

Unit 2 – Plants, Animals, Weather and Climate

2–7	7–11	11–14	14–19
Weather and climate	**Weather and climate**	**Weather and climate**	**Weather and climate**
Identifying and naming local/seasonal weather conditions *e.g. sun, rain, wind, snow*	Measuring temperature and spells of sun and rain *e.g. thermometer, clock, calendar readings*	Using a weather station *e.g. wind speed, wind direction, rainfall*	Safety precautions *e.g. frost, gales, ice, lightning, sunburn*
Making daily weather records *e.g. 'Monday: today it is cloudy'*	Maintaining weather charts over time *e.g. rain, sun, temperature and day length*	Recording local weather *e.g. prevailing winds, rainfall patterns*	Interpretation and use of weather forecasts *e.g. frost, wind damage, flood, sun, planning an outing*
Using weather pictures *e.g. clouds, fog, frost*	Using graphs and symbols *e.g. cloud, raindrop, sun, bar charts*	Recognising standard meteorological symbols *e.g. national weather maps*	Use of standard forecasts *e.g. newspaper, TV*
Climatic effects	**Climatic effects**	**Climatic effects**	**Climatic effects**
Naming weather conditions and sensory effects *e.g. hot, cold, wet, dry*	Seasonal weather effects *e.g. clothes for keeping warm/dry, growth in spring/leaf fall in autumn*	Local weather effects *e.g. wind damage, garden waterlogged, shade and shelter*	Global weather effects *e.g. drought, flood, crop failure*
Naming the seasons *e.g. spring, summer, autumn, winter*	Sequencing the seasons *e.g. months of the year, summer holidays, harvest*	World climate *e.g. rainforest, desert, tropics, arctic*	Environmental issues *e.g. desertification, water conservation, ozone depletion, global warming, acid rain*

format in Figure 5.1 is designed to cater for an all-age school. In practice, many schools will wish to plan over fewer age groupings than are suggested here and will wish to produce a two-stage, three-stage or four-stage version of the sheet.

Schools may also wish to adapt these progression planning and monitoring sheets in order to explore points of transition between early years and Key Stage 1; between departments within schools or between junior and senior schools; or between Key Stage 4 and school-based or college-based further education provision. We would suggest that collaboration between staff working across these points of transition can only enhance planning for continuity and progression.

Before moving on to discuss aspects of the medium-term planning process in more detail, we wish to follow up this section on progression and continuity with a few comments about breadth and balance. We will consider these issues both in terms of the whole curriculum and as a consideration within each subject-focused or integrated unit of work.

Breadth and balance

When medium-term plans for units of work in any given term are brought together, they may reveal an imbalance between the subjects. As we saw in Chapter 4, long-term planning may involve an alternating focus upon non-core foundation subjects. This may mean that a particular subject is taught in one term, but not in the next. Schools should be confident that this is an acceptable position, provided that planning sheets and records show that there is an appropriate balance across a broad curriculum over time.

Chapter 4 also noted that planning for cycles of units or modules will entail making decisions about those aspects of subjects that may be treated in depth as against topics covered in outline (Tate 1994; Stevens 1995). At the medium-term level of planning, teachers may wish to agree a commitment to cover the 'in depth' material as a minimum requirement for all pupils, working consistently towards achievement and progress. Those aspects that are to be covered in outline may be regarded as 'enrichment' activities, to be implemented or not at the discretion of the teacher. These may, indeed, offer opportunities for further achievement for some pupils who are able to move ahead but allow other pupils to continue to pursue basic skills and concepts in the context of new experiences.

Aspects of medium-term planning

We would hesitate to promote the use of any one format for medium-term planning. We do, however, suggest that there are a number of agreed elements or aspects of medium-term planning that should be represented in the documentation that emerges from this process. Many of these elements are exemplified in the format used in Figure 5.2. The details that locate this particular unit of work in relation to other aspects of the curriculum are provided at the top of the sheet. Here we are given a title for the module or unit of work; a cross-reference to the school's long-term planning; a subject focus for this unit; and any agreed and formal links with other areas of the curriculum. The sheet also allows for detailed cross-referencing to the programmes of study for the National Curriculum. After locating the unit of work in terms of the school and National Curriculum in this way, the format is structured around three aspects of planning that are here turned into questions in 'plain English':

- Objectives – 'What do I want pupils to learn?'
- Key activities and experiences – 'What will pupils do?'
- Assessment opportunities – 'How will I know when pupils achieve or make progress?'

This chapter goes on to explore these aspects of planning in more detail.

Objectives – 'What do I want pupils to learn?'

This aspect of the planning process entails thinking about and recording a set of intentions for pupils' learning in relation to a given area (or areas) of the curriculum over a specified length of time (for example, a term or half a term). It should be remembered that these should not be individual targets for learning such as would be found in an individual education plan (see Chapter 7). We suggest that medium-term plans should be designed to be used many times, year after year, with new cohorts of pupils as they arrive at the same point in the school's long-term curriculum plan. If this is to be the case, the objectives in a medium-term plan should describe the learning that a typical cohort of pupils in a given key stage or year group might achieve as a result of engaging with the unit of work.

If the unit of work is to ensure participation and achievement for pupils with special educational needs, then it is also important that the objectives are carefully differentiated to cover the typical range of prior experience and achievement that the school might expect from cohorts of pupils in the relevant age group. Figure 5.2 provides some examples of such objectives, ranging from the experiential (learning 'to respond to sensory events'); through learning that is related to the programmes of study at an early level (learning 'that switches can be used to control events'); towards more advanced attainments (learning 'to construct working circuits'). These object-ives reflect the fact that pupils in this school will be working in mixed, inclusive groupings; that school staff have anticipated this reality; and that all the pupils in the group, from those with the most profound difficulties in learning through to pupils achieving at or in advance of age-related expectations, will be expected to learn. The learning proposed in this section of the medium-term plan will relate to the subject focus of the unit of work. At the short-term stage of planning (see Chapter 6), individ-ual teachers will, of course, refine these objectives to make them precisely relevant to particular individual pupils and will integrate into their planning further targets that relate to the learning needs of specific individual pupils. At the medium-term planning stage, it is appropriate that the objectives devised should relate, in general terms, to the learning of a 'typical' or notional group of pupils and their experience of a particular unit of work.

Key activities and experiences – 'What will pupils do?'

The second key aspect of medium-term planning entails outlining some key activities or experiences with which pupils will engage in the course of this unit of work. It is important to note that this should not be an exhaustive set of detailed lesson plans. Again, we want to ensure that medium-term plans are used many times over the years in order to make the most of the considerable energy and expertise that is deployed in developing them. Medium-term plans should therefore provide staff with helpful guidance about activities and experiences that are characteristic of, or essen-tial to, a particular unit of work; for example, presenting a core set of activities and experiences that have been agreed by staff working in a planning group led by a subject co-ordinator. But medium-term plans should not be prescriptive nor should

Figure 5.2 Medium-term plan – 'Electricity' in Key Stage 1

Module Title: Electricity	Long-Term Map Reference: Science KS1 Summer A (a)	Subject Focus: Science	Links: Design and Technology

References to Programmes of Study: Science Key Stage 1 – Physical Processes
'Pupils should be taught about circuits involving batteries, wires, bulbs and other components; how a switch can be used to break a circuit'

Objectives *(What do I want pupils to learn?)*	Key Activities, Experiences and Organisation *(What will pupils do?)*	Assessment Opportunities *(How will I know when pupils achieve or make progress?)*
Pupils should learn: ■ that sensory events occur; to respond to sensory events; and to focus on sensory events; ■ that lights and sounds can change – 'on/off, loud/soft, bright/dim'; ■ that events occur in time – 'Now it's on/off'; ■ that events occur in time and space – 'Look over there'; ■ that switches can be used to control events; ■ that bulbs, batteries and wires can be joined to make circuits complete or incomplete; ■ to construct working circuits with bulbs, batteries and buzzers; ■ to 'name' (sign, symbol, eye point) sources of sound, light and movement.	Use dark room/light and sound room – regular sessions to explore lights and bubble tubes with small groups and/or individual pupils. Explore switched equipment in and around classroom/school – regular demonstrations and individual encounters with ICT, everyday objects, battery-operated toys, torches etc. Use electrically powered toys and equipment and compare with non-electrical – whole-class activity with battery-operated toys, bells, buzzers, spotlights, tape recorders etc. and guitars, candles, clockwork toys, push pull cars etc. Visit 'Launch pad' in Science Museum – class outing with 1:1 volunteer helpers and use of minibus. Construct circuits – demonstration by staff followed by small group tabletop activity to replace batteries, join wires, use clips, bulbs, switches etc. Extension – some pupils may wish to draw/record their circuits (Key Stage 2)	Pupils may: ■ react to sensory outcomes – bulbs, lighting, flashes, buzzers, movement etc. – P1; ■ attend to sensory outcomes in a focused way – look, listen, track etc. – P2; ■ participate in controlling events – operate switches etc. – P3; ■ anticipate outcomes – respond before, during and after sensory events – P4; ■ actively join in circuit-making – joining components etc. – P6; ■ communicate a response to changes in circuits – bulbs, lights, buzzers etc. – Level 1; ■ compare a working circuit with an incomplete circuit – Level 2.

Resources
(What will I need to use – what is available?)

Switch-controlled toys; battery-controlled toys; bulbs, wires, batteries, clips, buzzers; everyday electrical appliances, lights, torches, radios, tape recorders etc; soundbeam, keyboard, light and sound room, slide projector and OHPs; minibus for visits; variety of non-electrical sources of light, sound and movement.

they pre-empt decisions that should rightly be made by individual members of staff at the short-term planning stage.

In Figure 5.2, the activities and experiences proposed are varied. They include some practical classroom activity and a useful educational visit. They are well differentiated, so that pupils with the most profound difficulties in learning are actively involved (for example, in the strong sensory dimension that runs through the proposed activities) while other pupils consolidate prior learning and are encouraged to move towards higher attainment (for example, through the 'extension activity' drawing on programmes of study for Key Stage 2). The clear intention is that all pupils will be engaged, stretched and challenged by these activities and experiences. They are designed to ensure coverage of the content specified for this unit of work and to promote learning in relation to the objectives set. They will also support individual members of staff in developing their own detailed short-term plans, building on this framework of activities and experiences while developing flexible, creative and imaginative teaching ideas of their own.

Assessment opportunities – 'How will I know when pupils achieve or make progress?'

In our experience, there is often confusion between objectives and assessment opportunities. Objectives, we suggest, set out expectations or projected outcomes for learning that relate to the curriculum and/or learners' needs. Thus, using an example from Figure 5.2, teachers might expect pupils to learn about electricity and how it can be used; that electricity flows in circuits; and how to make an electrical circuit. These objectives summarise predicted or anticipated learning – but they do not necessarily tell us anything about what pupils will actually be able to do as a result of their learning. They leave open the question of how it will be possible to tell if a pupil has learned anything – and discovering what a pupil knows, understands and/or can do is the key task in assessment.

Sometimes there are very straightforward relationships between objectives and assessment opportunities. We will know that pupils have learned how to make an electrical circuit when they assemble wires, batteries and bulbs in such a way that the bulbs light up. In order to be certain that this scientific learning is secure, rather than the outcome of random joining, we might want to observe this behaviour several times. We might wish to insist that the pupils use slightly different pieces of equipment for some of these trials, so we can begin to be confident that they understand the general principle of circuit building rather than simply repeating one particular successful pattern. By observing behaviour in this way, we may begin to develop some insights into the pupils' learning 'about' electricity and the nature of circuits. But how will we assess pupils' knowledge and understanding about how electricity can be used? Again, we need to convert this rather abstract piece of learning into the kinds of pupil behaviours that we deem to be indicative of learning. So we may note, as an assessment opportunity, that we will watch out for pupils flicking light switches and looking for the lights to turn on and off; or for pupils turning the on/off switch on a radio when the volume control fails, by itself, to make music.

In Figure 5.2, assessment opportunities like these have been listed in advance so that staff are alerted to them and are ready to record significant pupil responses. The assessment opportunities here are linked to National Curriculum levels and P levels where appropriate, as we would recommend they should be in order to support summative assessment and reporting at the end of a year or key stage. They are also, as with the objectives and activities, carefully differentiated to ensure that all the pupils in the teaching group, from those with profound learning difficulties through to those who attain beyond age-related expectations, can be included as potential learners, active participants and significant achievers. We should also note that assessment using these opportunities is designed to be integral to the day-to-day flow of teaching and learning and not a separate process undertaken through a test or special activity. There may be a case to be made for offering specially designed assessment activities in certain key subjects at certain key times but, for the purposes of this book and the development of the schemes of work process, we suggest that assessment should be seen, for staff and pupils, as an integral and indivisible part of the flow of classroom activity.

It would be possible, of course, simply to do the teaching and to wait and see what happens – to allow the learning to reveal itself in pupils' responses and reactions to being taught. Sometimes, we propose, this is indeed a reasonable way in which to work. Usually, however, it is helpful to identify and note down projections about assessment opportunities at the planning stage in order to alert staff to behaviours and responses that are likely to be significant. This may be particularly important where schools decide to bring subjects together in linked units of work. Under these circumstances, it may be all too easy for the subject-specific significance of certain outcomes to be lost in the flow of integrated activity unless they are identified and highlighted at the planning stage. Setting down the opportunities for ongoing teacher assessment that planned activities offer in this way can make it possible to disentangle complexity and provide clarity of subject focus and precision with regard to level of outcome.

Schools working extensively with individual targets set in terms of the key cross-curricular skills (see Chapters 4 and 7) have found it useful to document the opportunities which implementing the programmes of study for the National Curriculum offers to make assessments of pupils' progress in these categories. Activities undertaken during a unit of science work can thus provide opportunities for pupils to solve problems, communicate or practise personal and social skills, for instance.

Other aspects of medium-term planning

A blank proforma, incorporating those key elements of Figure 5.2 described in detail above, is provided as Figure 5.3. Schools may wish to use this sheet as a basis for medium-term planning activities in curriculum working groups or, indeed, as a template from which to develop their own format for medium-term planning. As we have indicated, schools will have different needs and requirements in their medium-term planning and we would encourage colleagues to be constructive and creative in devising formats. Although we would recommend the use of broadly consistent formats for all phases of planning, we also acknowledge that different subjects and different age groups will impose different requirements on the planning process. Figure 5.2, for example, includes a section for listing resources – this may be particularly important in science, as in this case, where resources are centrally stored, or for history or geography units where staff may develop carefully compiled 'unit resource boxes'. In other areas of the curriculum or at other stages in the school age span, other priorities may need to be acknowledged in planning formats. The examples given as Figures 5.4 and 5.5 demonstrate how schools develop planning formats to meet their own needs while taking account of consistent core elements. They also illustrate the use of some

Figure 5.3 Blank format for medium-term planning

Class/KS:				MEDIUM-TERM ACTIVITY PLANNER	Term/Date:
Subject:			Links with:		Focus:
Unit of Work:			Programmes of Study:		

Key Objectives – Intended Learning Outcomes: *What do I want pupils to learn?*	Key Activities and Experiences – Organisation and Resources: *What will pupils do?*	Assessment Opportunities: *How might pupils respond? What might pupils achieve?*

Figure 5.4 Medium-term plan – geography in Key Stage 2

Using stories in geography

Title and Author of book:

The Jolly Postman – Janet and Alan Ahlberg

Suggested key stage: **Key Stage 2 – Year 3/4**
Links with scheme of work: **Key Stage 2, Year 3/4–Year A**
                                   'People who help us' and 'Our village'

Geographical Focus:

- Journeys and routes – following directions
- The community – people and services
- AT1 – geographical skills – mapping, making plans, landscape features and vocabulary
- AT2 – place – an opportunity to look at and compare with our own town

Learning Outcomes:

- To learn own address
- To develop enquiry skills – questioning, recording, sorting
- To develop geographical language, i.e. behind, over, river, road etc.
- To express a like/dislike for an environment
- To explore the use of maps and plans, and be able to follow simple directions
- To explore journeys and routes; how are they made and why?

Activities developed from the story:

- Visit a post office or interview a postal worker.
- Write letters to home and post them.
- Send letters to a neighbouring school and plan/follow their route.
- Bring in letters and postcards from home and locate on a map where they came from.
- Plan the jolly postman's route on a 2-D map and then make a 3-D map.
- Enquiry questions such as 'Would you like to live here? Why?'
- Look at plans and aerial views.
- Look at own journey to school. What do they pass on the way?
- Design own postage stamps.
- Discuss different jobs and roles in the community.

EXTENSION ACTIVITIES: Discuss reality of the location, i.e. witches and giants, make own books, send letters within school, role play a post office, weighing of parcels, sorting of parcels, look at envelopes, explore the different reasons why people need a postal service, the history of sending messages.

Additional and multi-sensory resources:

Post bag – parcels – postal worker's hat – wooden blocks (to make sound of letter through letter box) – teddy bear – witch's wig – small posting boxes. Postcards – letters – envelopes – bicycle bell – stamps to lick/taste.

Assessment opportunities: **Does the pupil know his own address? Can he state the town in which he lives? Can the pupil correctly identify a river, road, church on a simple pictorial map? Can the pupil make a simple journey/route following directions? Is the pupil able to post a letter independently?**

Figure 5.5 Medium-term plan for RE in Key Stage 3

Key Stage 3	Date: Autumn term	Long-Term Reference Year 7

Module Title: Festivals and Celebrations

References to Programmes of Study
There are as yet no National Curriculum Programmes of Study for RE

Differentiated Objectives (What do we want pupils to learn?)

Foundation (some students will)
- Listen to example of music from around the world
- Taste foods from around the world that are associated with festivals

Access (most students will)
- Learn that there are many children all around the world. Look at where they live, what they look like, what they wear, what they eat and how they feel
- Learn about some of the festivals around the world that involve children

Extension (a few pupils will)
- Identify specific foods, where in the world they come from and who eats them, e.g. rice, potatoes or baked beans
- Discuss similarities and differences between children from different areas of the world

Resources (What is available to use?)
Refer to the Christian box
Books –
Children Just Like Me (celebration)
W is for World (Oxfam publications)
Video – 'Wide World' episode from Dottie and Buzz (Stop, Look and Listen)
Any of the episodes from the Water, Moon, Candle, Tree and Sword series
Music – The Coca Cola song – Children of the World Unite, We Are Family
Hymns – 'He's got the whole world', 'You in your small corner', etc.

New/useful vocabulary
Rich, poor, similar, different, world, home, abroad

Key activities, experiences and organisation (What will pupils do?)

- Learn about children from different countries around the world demonstrating that there is wealth and poverty in all countries, e.g. Britain – Church of England; Thailand – Buddhist; Italy – Catholic; Israel – Jewish
- Examine where they live, in what sort of accommodation? What do they look like? What foods do they eat?
- Listen to a range of music from countries around the world
- Learn about some of the autumn/winter festivals around the world involving children, e.g. Trung Thu, El dia de muettos, Thanksgiving, Diwali, Hanukkah, St Lucia, St Nicholas and Christmas
- Learn about organisations which help children around the world – Oxfam, Save the Children, Barnardo's etc.
- Compare a specific aspect common to children around the world, e.g. footwear or food

Differentiated Assessment Opportunities (How will I know when pupils achieve/make progress?)

- Express a preference for a particular type of music, e.g. Caribbean
- Recognise that we all may look different but that we will all feel the same emotions
- Realise that children in all parts of the world 'celebrate'
- Realise that there are both rich and poor children all around the world in every country
- Compare similarities and differences among children from different named areas of the world

ICT opportunities
Use ICT programmes to look at similarities and differences

of a range of other elements in medium-term planning, which might include sections for:

- Time allocation – 'How many hours of teaching over how many weeks?'

- Resources – 'What will I need to use? What is available?'

- Vocabulary – 'What new language will pupils need to learn or use?'

- ICT – 'How will pupils use information and communication technology?'

- Differentiation – 'What will pupils learn, do or achieve at foundation, core or access and extension levels?'

- Organisation – 'How will I group pupils, support learning, deploy staff, use different environments, use a range of teaching methods etc?'

- Key skills – 'What opportunities does this scheme of work provide, in terms of planning, implementation and assessment, for teaching key skills in the context of subject-focused activity?'

- Evaluation – 'What worked well? What was less effective? What would I do differently another time?'

We would encourage schools to develop their own approaches to the development of medium-term plans using the ideas and processes set out here. As we said at the start of this chapter, it is often difficult to draw firm boundaries between long-term and medium-term planning. We further suggest that the interface between medium-term and short-term planning (see Chapter 6) is also complex and that some schools choose to explore these aspects of planning in close relationships with one another. In order to exemplify this possibility, we present, in the following sections, a discussion of modular planning that, in many senses, combines many of the things we wish to say about medium-term and short-term planning. Modules, in effect, offer staff an off-the-shelf set of outline lesson plans and substantially reduce the time that may need to be devoted to short-term planning.

Modules

In recent years the use of subject-focused modules has found favour in some schools (Rose 1994). Special schools, and particularly those with a predominantly secondary population, have found them helpful in making full use of teacher expertise in specific subjects and ensuring continuity, progression and full subject coverage. Some primary schools have found a modular approach useful for the delivery of a subject that does not easily fit into their customary planning methods. In such instances, a modular approach can help to ensure that the subject is fully covered and that all pupils receive their full entitlement to breadth in the curriculum.

For the school that intends to develop a modular approach, a number of questions arise concerning format and means of ensuring that the important aspects of assessment, continuity and progression are addressed. These issues will be addressed in this section, and working examples provided for teachers wishing to pursue this path.

What is a curriculum module?

A curriculum module defines the means by which the required content of part of a subject will be taught during a set period of time. It provides advice on teaching approaches, while recognising the importance of teacher autonomy, and ensures that the important elements of coverage and continuity are addressed. By developing a set format that is agreed by all staff, modules provide teachers with advice on activities to be undertaken, resources which may prove helpful, opportunities for assessment, and for cross-curricular coverage. Effective modules ensure that each lesson builds upon the knowledge, skills and understanding developed in the preceding lessons, and recognises that not all pupils will progress at the same rate, and that the achievements of pupils will vary. Strategies for differentiation (see Chapter 6) are established within the modular structure and consideration is given to means of providing appropriate access for pupils with special needs. Effective modules should therefore:

■ Define the purpose of each lesson, and its relationship to the other lessons in the module.

In order to address continuity and progression, a module must consist of a series of interrelated lessons, each building upon the skills, knowledge and understanding developed through the course of teaching. Progression will only be achieved if each lesson builds upon the work of those that preceded it, reinforcing the earlier work, as well as introducing new skills and concepts. A series of lessons, each related to a theme but ignoring the need for progression, will not assist pupils with special needs who need to develop ideas and reinforce learning over a period of time.

■ Indicate activities to be undertaken through the module.

With most schools now adopting cyclical models, and with much of the curriculum content defined by the National Curriculum, it is far more likely that courses developed this year will be used again in the future. This is where well-produced modules have definite advantages and the time spent on developing them can be justified. Over time, teachers become familiar with the format in which the school produces its modules. The indication of proven activities to be used with pupils, with a note of resource requirements, saves time in planning and preparation. The description of activities to be undertaken need not be comprehensive, but should rather be an indication of lesson content. It should be written in such a way that it does not inhibit individual teaching styles, while giving a clear path of progression through the lesson.

■ Indicate opportunities for assessment.

As we have said above, assessment should not be an 'add on' to teaching, but should rather build upon opportunities that exist in lessons for pupils to indicate what they have learned or achieved. When planning lessons, teachers should consider the assessment opportunities they are creating, and should look for indicators of learning which do not involve the production of contrived procedures. In some lessons, it is possible to identify numerous skills and a wide range of knowledge that could be assessed. Where this is the case, teachers should prioritise by assessing those outcomes that are most significant to the particular module; that are not addressed elsewhere; and that are most significant to pupils. Assessment for its own sake has limited value. Effective assessment is used to plan further development of pupils' learning. In the context of a modular approach, assessment should identify opportunities for learning within an activity which can then be built upon as the module progresses. The development of a set format, which identifies what is to be assessed, how achievement will be identified and how a pupil performed, is again a time-saving factor which should be built into the module planning.

- Indicate opportunities to provide access and differentiation for pupils with special needs.

Within each module lesson, teachers should plan and indicate where there may be a need to provide specific means of access to activities for pupils with special needs. This will often refer to individual pupils, who may require specialist equipment, or positioning, or a means of communication that will enable them to participate more fully in a lesson. When writing modules, teachers may consider the production of additional materials to be contained alongside the lesson plans, such as worksheets or self-evaluation forms, which enable pupils to access a lesson at differing levels (see Chapter 6).

- Provide cross-curricular references.

Even when working through a subject-based approach, most lessons will provide opportunities for addressing the key skills or the requirements of other subjects. Some indication of these when planning modules may encourage teachers to be aware of opportunities which could, in some instances, be overlooked. Producing lengthy lists of possible links to other subjects is not helpful as teachers will not have time to address these in any detail. It is far more helpful to indicate where lesson content will, of necessity, call upon knowledge or skills that may have been developed through other subjects and that can be either put to practical use during the lesson or reinforced through its content.

Figure 5.6 'Changes in materials' module

CURRICULUM MODULE TITLE: Changes in materials (SCIENCE AT3)

Lesson number 5 Ice cubes and insulation (1)

Equipment

Ice cubes, jars for the cubes, worksheets and pencils.

Activities

Pupils to place ice cubes in a variety of locations and to predict the time it will take for them to melt completely.

Pupils to choose locations, and to predict which will be the quickest to melt, and which the slowest, and to give approximate times.

Discuss reasons for pupils' predictions. Note what changes are involved, and what factors influence the rate of change.

Record results and complete worksheets.

Focus for assessment

Pupils' abilities in prediction.

Observation of change.

Access/differentiation

Two levels of worksheet

Some pupils to record results using stopwatches, others to use terms such as longest time and shortest time without using standard measures.

Cross-curricular references

Mathematics – Handling data

Module development in practice

To see how the development of curriculum modules can be undertaken in practice, examples have been included which should assist any school wishing to develop this approach.

Figure 5.6 is an example of a page from a science-focused curriculum module. It describes an activity to be undertaken by a group of pupils as part of an overall theme of changes in materials (science attainment target 3). In planning this lesson, the teacher has indicated the equipment that will be required; established opportunities for assessment; provided notes on access and differentiation; and indicated that a mathematical feature, handling data, is an essential part of the lesson. This format offers an easy-to-use approach to module planning and a blank for photocopying is included for use as Figure 5.13.

Figure 5.7 is an example of a worksheet produced to accompany the module lesson plan that we have just examined. Figure 5.8 provides another example, for a pupil who has more limited literacy skills. In this case, the worksheet makes use of *Writing with Symbols* (Widget 1994). It is important to recognise that, while both worksheets are valid and relate to the lesson content, they are not dealing with entirely the same aspects of the lesson. This would not, of course, be unusual where the teacher was working with a group of pupils with varying needs. These worksheets, produced at the same time as the lesson plans, are contained within the module alongside the relevant lesson page. Further worksheets, aimed at specific groups of pupils, may be added over time as the module is repeatedly used as part of the school's cyclical approach.

Figure 5.7 'Changes in materials' worksheet

> ### Changes in materials lesson 5
> ### Ice cubes and insulation

Where did you put your 4 ice cubes?

Ice cube 1

Ice cube 2

Ice cube 3

Ice cube 4

Which one did you think would be the slowest to melt?

How long did you think it would take to melt?

How long did it take to melt?

Which one did you think would be the quickest to melt?

How long did you think it would take to melt?

How long did it take to melt?

Write a few sentences about the changes to the ice cubes which took place.

Changes in materials lesson 5
Ice cubes and insulation

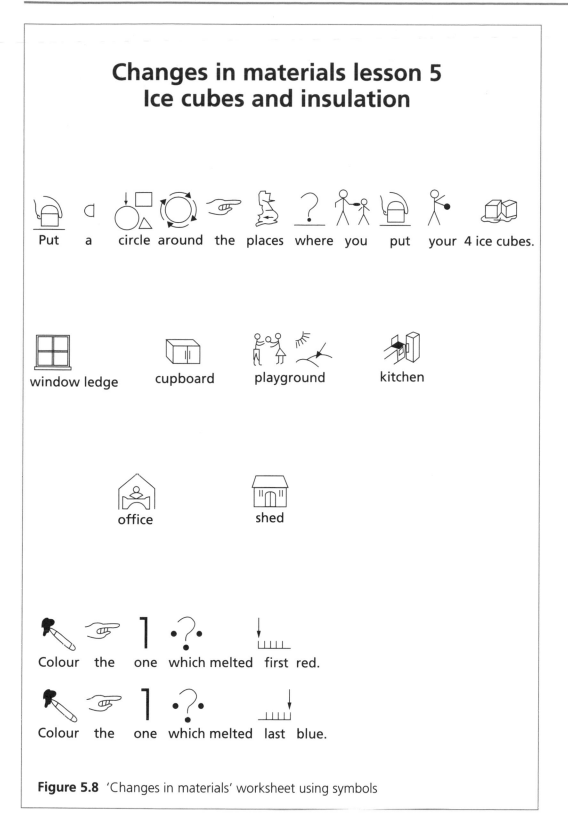

Put   a   circle around the places where you   put   your 4 ice cubes.

window ledge   cupboard   playground   kitchen

office   shed

Colour   the   one   which melted first red.

Colour   the   one   which melted last blue.

Figure 5.8 'Changes in materials' worksheet using symbols

Figure 5.9 'Changes in materials' assessment sheet

**Changes in materials lesson 5
Ice cubes and insulation (1)
Assessment Sheet**

Pupil's name   **Date**

Assessment focus
Pupil's ability to make predictions

Indicators
Pupil contributes predictions about which ice cubes will melt quickest, slowest, during discussion.
Predictions accompanied by reasoning, e.g. the ice cubes on the window ledge will melt quickly because of the heat from the sun.
Evidence through answers given on worksheets.

Assessment statement
————————was/was not able to make predictions based upon reasoning during the lesson.

Assessment focus
Pupil's skills in observing change

Indicators
A   Pupil able to indicate that ice cubes changed gradually from a solid state (ice), through a process of melting to a liquid state (water).
B   Pupil able to indicate the effects which different locations had upon the time which it took for ice cubes to melt.
Evidence through discussion, and through worksheets.

Assessment statement
————————was/was not able to observe changes to the ice cubes.
————————was/was not able to indicate the influence of different locations upon the ice cubes.

Figure 5.9 is an assessment sheet which accompanies the lesson (and, again, a blank is included for your use as Figure 5.14). This sheet refers to the assessment focus established for the lesson, with indicators for assessment opportunities and a box to contain a simple statement about the achievements of the pupil.

As has been emphasised, continuity and progression are important elements in the development of a modular approach. Figure 5.10 shows how the lesson that follows the one examined builds upon the skills and knowledge developed. The emphasis upon assessment is the same as for the earlier lesson, providing an opportunity for the teacher to make observations upon retention of learning and consistency. Similarly, the worksheets Figures 5.11 and 5.12 follow an established format, but develop further the themes started in the earlier lesson.

The examples provided here demonstrate one format for the development of a modular approach. Schools developing curriculum modules may adopt this format or may wish to modify it to suit their own needs. The development of modules should be seen as a complementary approach to others described in this book, and is certainly one which may be considered for schools wishing to follow a more subject-focused curriculum development path, perhaps one particularly suited to the needs and interests of older pupils. The advantages of a modular approach are as follows:

- Plans show a clear path of progression through a course related to a subject.

- Classroom management is made easier through the clear indication of resource needs and opportunities for assessment. Resources can be assembled before they are required and then stored for future use the next time the module is to be taught.

- After the initial work in producing the module, course content is established. This can be used and added to as required for future use.

- Staff, pupils and parents quickly become familiar with a set format which provides a means of planning and assessment that may then be easily incorporated into teacher records.

The following chapter, on short-term planning, continues many of the topics and themes that have been introduced in this chapter and goes on to show how priority areas of learning for individual pupils with special educational needs can be integrated into group activity focused on the curriculum.

Figure 5.10 'Changes in materials' module development

CURRICULUM MODULE TITLE:
Changes in materials (SCIENCE AT3)

Lesson number 6 Ice cubes and insulation (2)

Equipment
Ice cubes, jars for ice cubes, range of materials for insulation, including plastic, newspaper, cartridge paper, cloth (three different types), polystyrene. Scissors, worksheets, pencils, sticky tape, glue sticks.

Activities
Pupils to devise methods to make ice cubes melt more slowly in the same locations as used previously.
Discuss concept of a fair test with pupils, temperature in locations today may differ from last week.
Provide pupils with a range of materials to use, and encourage them to make predictions about insulation properties of these materials.
Use worksheets and produce charts to record results.

Focus for assessment
Pupil's abilities in prediction

Access/differentiation
Two levels of worksheet
Pupils to work in groups, with support given to pupils who have difficulties cutting materials. Classroom assistant to talk through last week's lesson with pupils who have difficulties retaining information.

Cross-curricular references
Mathematics – Handling data

Figure 5.11 'Changes in materials' further worksheet

> ## Changes in materials lesson 6
> ## Ice cubes and insulation
>
> **Which material did you think would work best as an insulator?**
>
> **Why did you think this would work best?**
>
> **Were you right?**
>
> **How long did it take for the ice cube to melt?**
>
> **Find your sheet from last week. How long did the ice cube in the same place take to melt last week?**
>
> **Can you think of anywhere in your home where insulation is used?**

Changes in materials lesson 6
Ice cubes and insulation

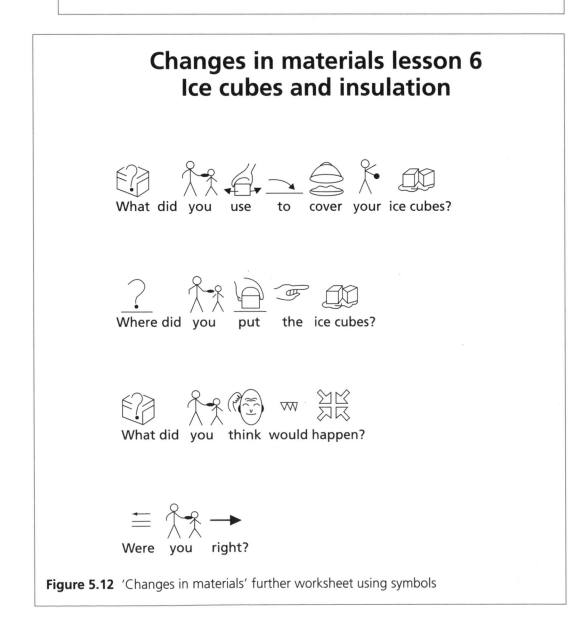

Figure 5.12 'Changes in materials' further worksheet using symbols

Figure 5.13 Blank module planning sheet

CURRICULUM MODULE TITLE:

Equipment

Activities

Focus for assessment

Access/differentiation

Cross-curricular references

Figure 5.14 Blank module assessment sheet

Module Assessment Sheet

Pupil's name   **Date**

Assessment focus

Indicators

Assessment statement

Assessment focus

Indicators

Assessment statement

Short-term planning 6

Short-term planning for pupils with special educational needs brings the ideas prepared in medium-term plans for curriculum-related group activity (see Chapter 5) into a dynamic relationship with the targets set out in individual education plans (IEPs) to address learning priorities for individual pupils (see Chapter 7). Where medium-term plans and IEPs are effective and of good quality, we would argue that detailed short-term lesson or activity planning in a written form is not necessary for every session of every week. This is especially true where teachers are experienced with both the subject matter they are covering and the pupil group they are teaching. For experienced members of staff, even the reworking and adaptation of tried and tested medium-term plans in order to meet the needs of a new year group of pupils (some of whom will, of course, bring with them new, short-term IEP targets and management challenges but all of whom will have fresh individual needs) may be an informal, internal, largely cerebral process. Indeed, we would argue that attention paid to formal short-term planning as new schemes of work are developed, and the adoption of selected, well-constituted specimen activity plans as exemplary materials within schemes of work documentation (as in the science module examples in Chapter 5), should mean that staff will not have to reinvent the wheel constantly.

On the other hand, staff working in specialist or inclusive settings should not expect to be able to deliver a standard syllabus year after year, term by term. Short-term planning in respect of pupils' changing individual needs and those precise strategies that will ensure access to the curriculum and achievement in response to learning opportunities should be seen as an ongoing requirement for all staff working with pupils with special educational needs.

Activity planning

As Sebba (1994) suggests, subject specialist teachers, subject co-ordinators, and, indeed, other interested and enthusiastic members of staff will generate a 'resource bank' of activity plans as they implement the units of work agreed upon during the long-term and medium-term planning phases. It will be useful to make a point of writing up and collating a range of these specimen plans as units of work are developed and implemented. Staff will be able to add to this collection as experience and evaluation indicate improvements, amendments or additions to the resource bank. We contend that such activity plans should not be seen as prescriptive or exclusively the 'right' way to approach aspects of teaching but should be presented, in a spirit of shared expertise and support, as useful ideas which have worked well in the past and which might be used as a stimulus for further development. They may be appended behind medium-term plans in schemes of work documentation and maintained under review as a portfolio of specimen solutions to the challenge of implementation (see Chapter 5).

Short-term plans may help staff to focus their thinking on a wide range of issues, in particular, how to:

- address individual pupils' targets and priorities for learning in curriculum-related group activity;
- differentiate activities successfully for a specific group of pupils;
- ensure meaningful access routes to curriculum content by generating extensions to the programmes of study;
- integrate cross-curricular elements in subject-focused teaching;
- create a balance between experiential, investigative styles of learning, routine acquisition and maintenance of skills, and activities which allow pupils to assimilate, consolidate or apply new understandings;
- plan for pupil collaboration and co-operative group work in balance with individual work and class activity;
- select appropriate resources and use them to best advantage in relation to specific aspects of a unit of work;
- manage time, staff, volunteers, equipment and space to the benefit of pupils and their learning;
- create opportunities to record achievement and assess pupil progress against individual targets and in relation to subject-specific aims.

Many experienced teachers, when planning work for new, unfamiliar groups of pupils, or coming to terms with subject content new to them, or when freshening up previously taught aspects of units of work in the light of evaluation, will want to continue to plan certain activities in some detail. Often such activity – a site visit, perhaps, or an in-school simulation; a major practical investigation or a dramatic presentation – will be the 'set piece' which provides the focus for a sequence of related, more routine activities or the culmination of a series of related sessions. There is no doubt that such selective planning will also enhance teaching and learning during the satellite sessions which enable pupils to prepare for and follow through the experiences gained during well-planned, central activity.

Some examples may serve to illustrate the issues. Figure 6.1 shows a lesson planning sheet which allows the teacher to prepare for a single science lesson – one of a series of such sessions outlined in medium-term plans for units of work (see Chapter 5). She considers pupil groupings and broadly differentiated activity (see below in this chapter). She thinks about how she means to deploy staff and volunteers and she makes a note of the resources she will require for the lesson. She uses the final section of the sheet to make notes, during or after the event, about the responses made by individual pupils. She may use these records of learning outcomes later to evaluate the effectiveness of her teaching; to reconsider the pupil groupings she has set up; and to monitor pupil progress and achievement (see Chapter 7).

In Figure 6.2, the teacher has planned a series of mathematics lessons. Specific mathematical objectives, differentiated from P7 to Level 2, are given at the top of the sheet. A selection of the students' individual targets, focusing on those issues that can be addressed in mathematics lessons, are then set out. Next a series of planned group activities are detailed, with notes, in the middle columns, about how these activities will be differentiated (see below). In the right-hand column, the teacher begins to make notes about the responses that the students make as the series of lessons proceeds.

Figure 6.1 Lesson plan for science

Lesson plan			
Subject: Science	**Date:** 2	**Week:** 9	**Class:** JS

What do you want the pupils to learn?

Group 1 & 2: that some items conduct electricity

Group 3: work on making circuits to work buzzer or switch

What the pupils are actually going to do:

Group 1 & 2: experiment and test different items to see if they conduct electricity or not; put into sets; observe properties of items in sets

Group 3: further work on simple circuits; use bulb, switch, buzzer; answer questions as they work

Resource needs:

Electricity resource box

Any necessary classroom organisational issues:

Group 1: MB, FP;   Group 2: HG, LM, BC;   Group 3: JH, WD, KT

Groups 1 & 2 work with CA and college student

Group 3 work individually, supervision from JS and work experience student

Learning outcomes:

Group 1: FP realised that 'metal' conducts, predicted 'make it work' each time, carried out own checks on circuit connections when testing

Group 2: LM absent. BC very experimental, eventually realised that 'metal' objects 'worked', needs more experience

Group 3 need more work on circuits: KT still unsure; JH competent most of time & enjoyed experimenting; WD had fine motor problems but said and gestured wires to connect

Figure 6.2 Activities plan for mathematics

SUBJECT: Mathematics	TOPIC/FOCUS: Money	CLASS: KS3L1 group
TEACHER: Dave	TERM: Summer	1st HALF-TERM
LEARNING OBJECTIVES	To recognise and name/identify all coins. P7 To recognise and name/identify all notes. P7 To understand the sequences and processes necessary for shopping. L1 To be able to demonstrate that 2 × 1p = 2p. L1 To demonstrate awareness of coin equivalencies. 2p 5p 10p. L1 To give change from 5p and 10p coins. L1 To identify which coin is worth more from a choice of at least 2. L1 To demonstrate awareness of coin equivalencies 20p 50p £1. L2	

STUDENTS' IEP AND/OR CURRICULUM TARGETS

Name	Ellie	Jack	Naima	Andrew
Target	To recognise, name and identify all coins	To recognise, name and identify all coins	To demonstrate awareness of coin equivalences. 2p 5p 10p	To identify which coin is worth more from a choice of two

Activity	Teaching Activities (Resources and use of support staff)	All students will:	Most students will:	Some students will:	Evaluation
			Differentiated learning outcome		
1	Coin recognition/matching all coins to £1. Worksheet – find the correct amount of money, use sticky coins	Have experience of handling coins	Recognise some of the coins with support	Recognise all the coins they are offered	Ellie all coins up to 20p. Naima remembered how many pence in £1. All students were engaged, motivated by activity
2	Use coins in role play activities in exchange for goods. Use worksheets to reinforce the concepts – shopping sheet: work out the cost of items identified up to 25p	Have experience of using coins to exchange for goods	Will be able to find the correct amount of money to exchange for the goods with support	Will be able to find the correct amount of money to exchange for the goods independently	Good activity enjoyed by all. Nobody was able to find the correct amount of money without help
3	Money lotto game – complete worksheets to reinforce skills. Money recognition activity	Have experience of handling coins	Recognise some of the coins with support	Recognise all the coins they are offered	
4	Counting in 2s using pennies. Complete worksheets to reinforce skills taught	Have experience of counting in 2s	If prompted be able to count on in 2s	Will be able to count on in 2s independently	
5	Introduce paper money. Complete worksheets to reinforce concepts taught	All will have experience of handling paper money	Will be able to identify notes with support	Will be able to identify notes independently	

Figure 6.3 Activities plan for history

Activities planning sheet		

Date: Jan to Feb   **Key Stage:** 3   **Class:** 9B

Title: Roman Empire (History)

Week:	Plan:	Reality:
1	Quick revision of timeline Map of Roman Empire; Zig Zag 1	Revision of timeline Map of Roman Empire; Latin names Extracts from Zig Zag 1
2	Pompeii; Zig Zag 3 Roman economy	Zig Zag 3; how do we know about Pompeii? matching Roman & modern objects; sorting coins
3	Being an archaeologist handling session prepare for museum visit	Practise handling artefacts observation & discussion watch Time Teams
4	Bedford Museum blanket dig observe & record artefacts	Blanket dig at Bedford museum handling Roman objects question curator
5	Plaster casting Guiseppe Fiorelli	Recall museum trip observation, drawing use of recording sheets
6	Revision and assessment	Assessment Now and Then video

Key concepts:	Resources:
place events, people and changes within a chronological framework (KS3)	Zig Zag video
	Time teams video
investigate independently using artefacts, pictures, photos and film, buildings and sites (KS3)	Bedford museum
	Library Project collection
government, state, empire, republic, peasantry, trade, dictatorship (KS3)	Roman resource file

Figure 6.3 shows a plan for a half-term series of history lessons in Key Stage 3. This teacher again records the aims of the sessions, as key concepts to be studied, and notes the resources required. This sheet then charts the difference between planned activity, in the left-hand column, and what the pupils actually experienced, on the right. At first things proceed more or less according to plan, with the teacher noting particular aspects which have caught the pupils' imaginations (Latin names and Roman coins, for instance). However, the blanket dig in week 4, where pupils lift layers of blankets and 'unearth' ever older items as they move down through the layers, proves to be such an exciting activity in its own right that the planned recording of artefacts is not carried out. This work is completed the following week back at school and the plaster casting is postponed for another session. These notes, taken alongside records of the responses of individual pupils, will constitute both a valuable record of experience for this whole class (see Chapter 7) and a means of evaluating the unit of work when the time comes to teach this study unit again.

We will now turn to a more detailed exploration of some of the planning issues raised by these examples.

Differentiation

Differentiation is one important aspect of short-term planning, whether formal or informal – indeed, many commentators argue that differentiation is the key to ensuring access to the curriculum for pupils with special educational needs (Carpenter 1992). Any or all of the levels of planning we have discussed in this book so far will benefit from being well differentiated. As we have seen, various review processes, revisions and statements about inclusion have brought the theoretical ideal of a differentiated National Curriculum within the grasp of all pupils. Working at the earliest levels of achievement within Key Stage 3 can now be a practical reality (see Chapter 1).

We have also explored the notion of units of work, differentiated in terms of sequence and progression for particular age groups of pupils (see Chapters 4 and 5). We now wish to examine differentiation at the level of lesson, task, activity or session planning – at the interface between the proposed curriculum and the learning needs of individual pupils. Ann Lewis (1992) offers a thorough analysis of a range of possible varieties of differentiation and the following material borrows heavily from her ideas. Lewis proposes that adjusting tasks to the various interests, needs, aptitudes, experiences and previous achievements of diverse groups of pupils may entail thinking about:

- **content** – so that pupils work on various aspects of the same subject matter, for example, a reading activity focusing upon social sight recognition for some pupils and phonic word attack skills for others;

- **interest** – ensuring that activities have relevance to pupils' own experience and sources of motivation;

- **level** – enabling pupils to work on similar concepts at levels that reflect their previous achievements, so that, in the course of a lesson about plants as living things, one pupil may confirm the idea that plants need water in order to live while a second pupil comes to understand that the roots of a plant draw moisture up out of the soil;

- **access** – so that material is presented to pupils through various modes, whether aural, visual, tactile, concrete, symbolic, linguistic or via information technology;

- **structure** – whereby work may be presented, for instance, in small, developmentally sequenced, subject-specific steps for some pupils and in conceptually holistic, integrated chunks for others;

- **sequence** – allowing pupils access to material in varying orders which may be planned in advance or determined spontaneously by pupil preference;

- **pace** – encouraging pupils to work through material at varying speeds, again either because work is presented to them at different rates or because they are encouraged to determine their own preferred pace;

- **response** – acknowledging that pupils will respond to similar activities in varied ways, either because the teacher has planned to request different outcomes from different individual pupils or because pupils spontaneously respond in different ways;

- **staff time** – allowing individual pupils different amounts and qualities of staff support, varying from intensive 1:1 input, through pauses permitting delayed responses, to occasional guidance for pupils working essentially independently;

- **teaching style** – ensuring that pupils experience a range of approaches to teaching from didactic classroom presentations, through investigative, experiential fieldwork, to discursive tutorials;

- **learning style** – giving pupils opportunities to respond to teaching in a variety of ways, whether by listening passively, participating actively in explorations and discoveries, or taking the lead in solving problems;

- **grouping** – offering a balance of individual, paired, group, class, departmental and whole-school learning experiences.

It is worth noting here that these forms of differentiation can be distinguished broadly in terms of differentiated input and outcome. Further, many of these strategies can encourage both detailed teacher planning and pupil self-differentiation. Clearly, effective planning for differentiation often depends upon accurate assessment of pupils' prior achievements; considered diagnosis of future learning needs; and tightly focused target setting, although this may itself be a process that is negotiated between teacher and pupil (see Chapter 7). At other times, however, staff will wish to allow pupils to self-differentiate, particularly where tasks are open-ended or investigative, encouraging pupils to develop their own access strategies in shared activities and to pursue varied outcomes. Staff in these instances should be prepared to observe pupils' approaches to problem-solving and exploration and to record the resulting differentiated responses.

There is no suggestion here that all of these aspects of differentiation should be called into play in every lesson. This is not a checklist of imperatives but a suggested range of possibilities. Staff will need to decide when to control differentiation and when to facilitate pupil-directed learning. Different sessions and subjects will lend themselves to various forms of differentiation according to the curricular aims that apply and the group of pupils involved. Individual teachers or teachers working in teams may wish to work through some of these ideas, however, as an aid to planning particular sessions or sequences of sessions. Subject co-ordinators may introduce the notion of a differentiation audit (Galloway and Banes 1994) to colleagues as part of their responsibility for monitoring curriculum implementation (see Chapter 9). This set of ideas will then constitute a useful prompt for focused discussion and an agenda for development. Figures 6.4 and 6.5 offer a handout on differentiation and a blank format which staff may wish to photocopy for note-taking in these discussions.

Figure 6.4 Twelve kinds of differentiation

content
pupils work on various aspects of the same subject matter

interest
activities reflect pupils' own interests/experiences

pace
pupils work through material at varying speeds; work is presented at varying rates

sequence
pupils dip into material in varying orders – planned? self-selected?

level
pupils work on similar concepts at different levels, reflecting previous achievements

access
material is presented to pupils through varying modes – aural, visual, tactile, concrete, IT, symbols, linguistic

response
pupils respond to similar activities in varying ways – may be planned (teacher requests varied outcomes) or spontaneous (pupils' responses vary)

structure
work presented in small, developmental steps or in conceptually related chunks; subject-specific or integrated

teacher time
1:1 time with teacher; time allowed for responses; additional support time

teaching style
didactic? investigative? discursive?

learning style
listening? exploring? problem-solving?

grouping
individual? pairs? groups? class? whole school or department?

(*Adapted from* Lewis 1992)

Group work

We have noted the use of group work, considered in relation to other forms of pupil grouping, as one aspect of differentiation. Many activities proposed by the National Curriculum actively require pupils to work together in groups (Byers 1994b) and it is now accepted that learning to work in a range of groupings is an important part of education for all pupils. The debate about group work has been pursued in detail elsewhere (McCall 1983; Rose 1991; Sebba *et al.* 1993). Suffice it to say here that teachers

Figure 6.5 Planning for differentiation

Session focus:

| content | response |

| interest | structure |

| pace | teacher time |

| sequence | teaching style |

| level | learning style |

| access | grouping |

will wish to consider the purpose and constitution of groups in their planning. For example, groups may be:

- homogenous – a set of pupils whose learning needs are broadly alike and who are expected to be able to work together on a shared task at a comparable rate and towards similar outcomes;
- heterogeneous – a mixed grouping of pupils who bring significantly varied prior experiences, achievements and aptitudes to a shared task.

Many schools, faced with the challenge of teaching classes of pupils with widely differing prior achievements, choose to adopt a strategy whereby pupils with similar needs are grouped together. In some instances, pupils are withdrawn from class in small groups to work together in a geographical location that is separate from their peers. The rationale for this strategy is that pupils working at similar levels learn together effectively and that those pupils with the most complex needs do not impede the progress of the rest of the class. There may, indeed, be a justification for creating homogenous sets of pupils, both those experiencing difficulties in achieving and those whose rapid prior progress indicates the need for enrichment activity, on occasion. These sorts of temporary groupings for specific activities should not be confused with permanent forms of segregation. Streamed groupings deny the benefits that a well-differentiated approach may offer to all pupils and fail to recognise that pupils require opportunities to play a variety of roles in learning situations. The line between differentiation and discrimination can, at times, become somewhat thin (Hart 1992) and teachers need to consider with great care their reasons for grouping pupils. Research in the area of collaborative learning does, in fact, suggest that all pupils, both the high achievers and those experiencing difficulties, make the greatest progress, both academically and socially, when working in fully integrated groups (Swing and Peterson 1982; Johnson and Johnson 1983; Slavin 1988). Indeed, we know many colleagues who argue that teaching the highest achieving pupils in groups with those who experience the most severe difficulties provides the best teaching and learning opportunities for all. However, making the most of opportunities to work in this way demands skill and careful planning. The following ideas may support staff in developing more effective group work.

Jigsawing

It may be possible to focus the differentiation more tightly within groups by allocating information, materials, resources and responsibilities to particular pupils or, indeed, by inviting the pupils to make their own decisions about their individual roles in the group. This technique has been referred to as 'jigsawing' (Rose 1991) and may be used to:

- promote the development of new skills, concepts, knowledge and understanding;
- encourage the maintenance, consolidation, demonstration in new contexts and generalisation of existing skills, concepts, knowledge and understanding.

Jigsawing has been used most successfully as a means of addressing the individual needs of pupils in group teaching situations. It has been particularly helpful to those teachers planning activities to include pupils with a wide range of special educational needs.

In jigsawing, the individual components of an activity are identified and the needs of pupils matched to these components. The emphasis upon planning has two main thrusts:

- to encourage pupils to work collaboratively, and develop their skills of interaction and sociability;

- to ensure that all pupils participate at an appropriate level, and that their individual needs are addressed.

This approach can be best illustrated through an example of its use. This example was produced by teachers on a SENSE curriculum management course in Bradford. Figure 6.6 lists a class of Key Stage 2 pupils who attend a school for pupils with severe learning difficulties. These pupils have a wide range of needs and characteristics, including profound and multiple learning difficulties, sensory impairments and difficulties on the autistic spectrum. Such a mix of pupils has become increasingly common in special schools in recent years. The class has been asked, as part of a technology lesson, to make a guy for the coming school Bonfire Night celebrations.

Figure 6.6 Characteristics of pupils

Characteristics of Pupils in the Group and Priorities for Technology Sessions

Sanjay. Has cerebral palsy. Limited movement of limbs. Left hand slightly easier than right. Poor distance vision.
Individual priorities. Co-operation with an adult in practical activities.

Susan. Has good levels of verbal communication but poor concentration. Behaviour can be difficult when challenged or if she does not wish to co-operate.
Individual priorities. Sharing materials with other pupils. Counting to ten.

Jenny. Proficient Makaton user. Likes to please. Easily distracted and rarely settles to an activity for more than a few minutes.
Individual priorities. Improved pencil control. Increased attention to task.

Neil. Profound and multiple learning difficulties. Very sociable. Very stiff arms, but developing grasp.
Individual priorities. Extending arms to reach for objects. Maintaining visual attention to objects placed in front of him.

Paul. Autistic tendencies. Level of co-operation variable. Enjoys mechanical/repetitive activities. Unpredictable behaviour. Good understanding of language but no speech.
Individual priorities. To remain in the room throughout a 20-minute activity. To complete a fine motor task lasting five minutes.

Mike. Developing Makaton user. Good concentration. Improving motor skills, eager to please, but easily frustrated if success does not come quickly.
Individual priorities. To improve control in tool use – pencil, scissors, brushes. To increase Makaton vocabulary related to technology lessons and to improve consistency in signing.

Judy. Withdrawn pupil who likes to work alone. Does not like adult intervention. A few spoken words. Good language comprehension but very stubborn.
Individual priorities. To change activities without losing temper. To participate as part of a group. To use please and thank you consistently.

Alan. No speech. Very passive and difficult to motivate. Good visual skills. Enjoys company of peers, but not often willing to co-operate in group activities.
Individual priorities. To share materials with peers. To remain on task for five minutes. To complete a visual activity alone.

Staff have identified the individual priorities to be addressed for particular pupils during technology lessons. In some instances these can be seen to have a social emphasis, while in other cases the priorities are more closely related to an academic curriculum. The challenge for staff is to plan an activity to encourage collaborative learning, providing access for all to designing and making while addressing some of the individual priorities established for specific pupils.

Figure 6.7 gives the chart used to plan the activity. In column one, the making of a guy has been divided into three parts. These parts consist of a series of activities which, when combined, will result in the production of the guy. The first group involves three pupils in choosing clothes and stuffing these with paper to make the guy's body. The second group is concerned with joining the parts of the guy together. The third group is producing a mask for the guy. The activity in itself is nothing unusual and, given the task to produce a guy, it is likely that most teachers would adopt a similar approach.

In column two, consideration has been given to the way in which pupils will be matched to the three activities. Recognition is given to the individual priorities set for pupils, along with physical needs and the level of support required. It can be seen, for instance, that Mike's improving motor skills are being addressed by encouraging him to use scissors. Susan's numeracy requirements have been considered and related to her part of the activity, and an opportunity has been created to address Neil's physical needs.

In order to be a group activity, rather than a collection of individual tasks, opportunities for collaboration need to be provided. In the second group, Susan and Paul are being encouraged to assist each other by holding the material taut while their partner sews. In the third group, a collective decision between Mike and Judy is

Figure 6.7 Jigsawed group activity

Making a guy for Bonfire Night

ACTIVITY	PUPILS	ASSESSMENT FOCUS
Pupils choosing clothes for the guy. Tying ends of arms and legs of clothes. Stuffing clothing with paper.	Alan to match clothes to pictures. Neil and Sanjay to be helped to screw up newspaper and stuff it into clothing.	Neil's ability to reach for paper and take paper from an adult.
Pupils using large sewing needles with string to join parts of the guy.	Susan and Paul to complete sewing. Paul to thread needles. Each pupil to hold material in place while the other sews.	Susan's ability to count (stitches) to ten, and to indicate more and less (number of stitches).
Pupils designing a mask for the guy. Choosing materials and making the mask.	Jenny to draw design. Mike to cut out materials and to give these to Judy, with Judy to decide where they should go on the mask. Judy to stick materials to mask.	Mike's use of scissors to cut along a straight line drawn on stiff material (using large scissors).

required before Judy completes her part of the task. The three groups are interdependent. The activity cannot succeed unless each group completes its part of the process. This means that opportunities exist for pupils to share their work and for the teacher to encourage communication and co-operation between the groups.

Teachers using the jigsawing approach need to be aware of the 'Blue Peter' factor. Because the groups are dependent upon each other, and not all will work at the same pace, it is necessary to prepare some of the work beforehand in order that pupils are not waiting too long for the earlier parts of the process to be completed. In the example given here, group two require some sewing work before group one have finished their part of the task.

Column three of the chart recognises that opportunities exist to assess the progress which some pupils are making in relation to their individual priorities. It also acknowledges that it is not practical to expect that every pupil's progress will be assessed during a lesson and that it is more realistic to concentrate only upon two or three pupils (see Chapter 8).

Planning for group activity in this way is a relatively simple process. When used consistently, it has the advantage of identifying, before the lesson, those parts of an activity that will be most readily addressed by individual pupils. It also enables the teacher to ensure that established individual priorities are considered during each lesson.

It is not suggested that all pupils in the example given, or in any other jigsawed activity, will participate for the whole session. It is recognised that different pupils have varying attention spans and that, in some instances, physical needs will restrict the length of participation. Planning in this way does ensure that the opportunities to make best use of limited participation, by matching needs to the activity, can be taken. In the example given, Alan's priority of remaining on task for five minutes can be addressed in the activity matched to his need. He is making a contribution to the lesson by identifying clothes to be used for the guy but his withdrawal, if necessary, after five minutes will not totally disrupt the group.

Jigsawed activities do not have to be broken down into three groups. Some activities lend themselves more easily to four groups, or in some cases, just two. Much will depend upon what is most easily managed in the class situation, and the number of staff available to assist with the approach. Figure 6.8 provides a blank chart for planning jigsawed activities and for identifying the individual pupil priorities that will be taken into account.

Clearly, jigsawed activity may be planned to encourage a mix of new endeavour and familiar activity. It is worth noting, however, that learning to collaborate may itself constitute a fresh challenge for many pupils, suggesting that this may be a good time to rehearse established skills and that groups working on new areas of learning may require increased staff support.

Envoying

Envoying, among other group work approaches that have proved useful for involving pupils with special educational needs, can be of particular use when addressing communication difficulties. This approach has been successfully deployed in a number of primary schools.

In envoying, a pupil is used as a carrier of information (envoy) between groups of pupils working on different aspects of a related task. In our example, pupils are working on the production of a brochure to advertise the Great Exhibition of 1851 as part of a Victorian history study unit. One group is investigating the latest inventions and

Figure 6.8 Blank chart for planning jigsawed group activity

ACTIVITY	PUPILS	ASSESSMENT FOCUS

industrial developments of this period, while another is considering the layout and format of the brochure. An envoy, or series of envoys, will be used to carry information from one group to the other to help the groups to co-operate in the overall planning of the brochure (see Figure 6.9 with a blank version for use by readers given as Figure 6.10).

One of the envoy roles is clarified in Figure 6.11. For a pupil with communication difficulties working alone, this may prove to be a daunting task. Support can be provided by pairing pupils for a single envoy role. In the example given here, Nigel is expected to report on only one piece of information. He is encouraged to use both written and pictorial information for support, and has been provided with an opportunity to rehearse his role with Rachel. The role played by Rachel needs to be carefully defined. She should be there as a support but not to take over the responsibilities given to Nigel. She should also be able to prompt him should he have difficulties in providing information. As Nigel gains in confidence in these sorts of roles, the amount of information that he carries can be increased and the support provided by one of his peers gradually diminished.

Some pupils' communication skills may be supported by the use of assistive information technology; through a communication board; or through the use of a symbol or signing system. Confidence in communication, and an understanding of the importance of interaction with a group, will only be achieved if pupils with special educational needs are given an equal opportunity to participate fully in roles like these.

Whichever approaches to promoting group work and interaction are developed in schools, teachers must be aware that, for all pupils, the skills necessary to participate as part of a group need to be learned. Both envoying and jigsawing have a proven worth in promoting group work, but both take time to establish and success in their use will seldom be achieved immediately. A key role for staff should be in the promotion of social interaction among pupils and the capacity to work with others. This will not be achieved through the perpetual use of individual teaching sessions. The development of effective group work strategies is essential if this goal is to be attained.

Staff interested in sharing views about group work may like to contact the Collaborative Learning Project at 17, Barford Street, London N1 0QB.

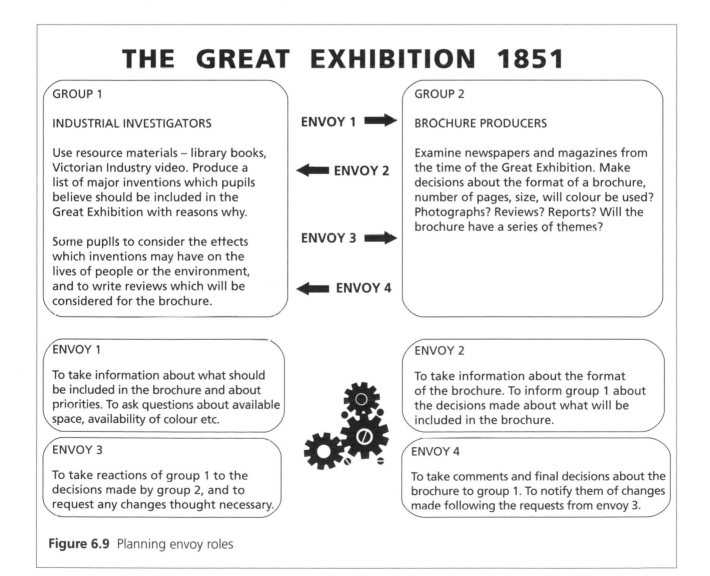

Figure 6.9 Planning envoy roles

Figure 6.10 Envoy planning sheet

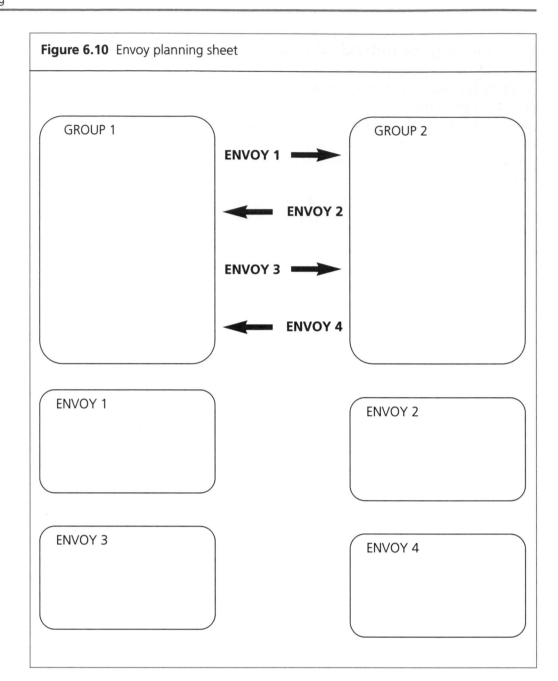

Figure 6.11 Envoying examples

THE GREAT EXHIBITION 1851

Envoy 2
To take information about the format of the brochure. To inform group 1 about the decisions made about what will be included in the brochure.

Nigel to act as envoy 2, but to be assisted by Rachel. Nigel to report on just one detail of the decision made about format. Use pictures for cue if necessary, and written notes. Nigel to rehearse his report to Rachel before going to group 1.
Rachel to conduct report on other points as envoy 2.

Planning for individual pupils

Planning that takes account of individual needs should be an integral part of the short-term planning process for pupils with special educational needs. Short-term planning may then take account of both subject-related targets (such as demonstrating an ability to use historical sources to draw conclusions or recognising some of the different ways in which musical sounds are made) and cross-curricular aspects of the curriculum such as the key skills (QCA/DfEE 2001a, 2001b). Many schools are finding that progression, continuity and relevance are enhanced for individual pupils when targets in IEPs are set in terms of key cross-curricular skills and pursued in the context of subject-related activity. This constitutes a truly integrated approach (Byers 1992) whereby pupils are offered access to activity founded in the programmes of study for the subjects of the National Curriculum and, at the same time, make progress towards highly individualised targets devised in response to honest perceptions of priority need (see Chapters 2, 4 and 7).

SCAA (1996) offers a pair of examples bringing together many of these principles. These examples provide brief pen portraits of two pupils with special educational needs, Natalie and Adil, and the contexts in which they undertake their learning. We have adopted a similar format in Figure 6.12 to give an account of Jamie's experience in a modern foreign languages lesson. It is worth noting here that Jamie learns in an inclusive mainstream school, although he does not attend all the modern foreign languages sessions provided for his age peers – he is included in those activities in which his needs can be most successfully met. Whatever the school setting, we would argue that it is appropriate for pupils with learning difficulties to spend most of their school time working with their age peers in order to enable them to be fully included in the curriculum on offer in their school. We also acknowledge that it is appropriate for some pupils to spend some time working with specialist staff in specialist environments in order to take account of their particular individual personal,

---

Figure 6.12 Jamie's IEP targets and lesson plan

Jamie is in Year 11. He has cerebral palsy, learning difficulties and he uses a voice synthesiser to communicate. On Wednesday morning, he joins his peers for a lesson in modern foreign languages. On this occasion, his peers are adopting the roles of staff members and customers to simulate interactions in a street cafe in France. Jamie's task is to participate as a customer. The teacher wants all interactions to take place in the target language. Jamie's voice synthesiser is programmed with appropriate French phrases.

Individual priorities	Experience – context	Responses – achievement
■ to initiate and turn-take in interactions ■ to look at and point to items he wants ■ to indicate choices using gesture, symbols and IT	Group role play in a cafe simulation, chequered table cloths, accordion music, smells of coffee, hot bread, pastries. Students to order foods, offer courtesies and greetings in French.	Jamie looks at the counter with prompt. Responds to choice between coffee & hot chocolate using his voice synthesiser – he eye points and activates 'café, s'il vous plait'.
Establish new priorities leading to revised short-term targets and long-term goals for individual pupils.	**Review curriculum plans** by evaluating and refining sequences of activity, schemes of work & policy.	**Report on pupil progress** by noting achievements in National Curriculum and other programmes.

paramedical, therapeutic and educational needs. These sessions will help the young people concerned to be more effectively included with their peers for the majority of the time.

In Figure 6.12, an introduction to Jamie, including an outline of his participation in one particular scheme of work, is given in the row that runs across the page. In the left-hand column under this pen portrait, a set of individual targets, drawn from Jamie's IEP and the annual review process, is given in a bullet-pointed list. In the middle column, the activity in one particular lesson, related to the scheme of work alluded to in the pen portrait, is described. In the right-hand column, Jamie's responses to the activity in which he has been engaged are recorded. A brief analysis of this vignette may help to secure its significance.

Jamie's IEP targets suggest that he is working on three key areas: initiation and turn-taking in interactions with other people; eye pointing (looking at) or finger pointing to items he wants; and making choices by gesturing, pointing to symbols or activating his voice synthesiser. It might be possible to link these targets to subject areas (initiating interactions linked to English and using a voice synthesiser linked to information and communication technology, for example). However, we suggest that it would be more accurate, relevant and appropriate to propose that they relate to key skills (in this case, communication, information technology and working with others) and other cross-curricular priorities for Jamie, including the development of personal and social skills. We would also suggest that Jamie is fully and meaningfully involved in activities that relate to the school's scheme of work for modern foreign languages. Indeed, this role play activity has been designed around Jamie's involvement. Placing the pupil with the most profound difficulties at the very centre of planned activity is a technique we have encountered many times and is a strategy for promoting inclusion that we would endorse. In this lesson, Jamie responds in very clear ways. His teachers, and most people who have been exposed to this example, agree that he has made progress in relation to his IEP targets. He has taken his turn in a purposeful interaction. He looks at the items on offer in the simulated cafe and indicates his choice using both eye pointing and information technology. These achievements are worthy of being recorded and may help staff to refine and refocus Jamie's future IEP targets. We would also like to suggest that Jamie's achievements are significant in terms of modern foreign languages in the National Curriculum. He has been involved in communicating in the target language in pairs and groups; using the target language in the context of everyday activities and personal and social life; and, arguably, developing cultural awareness – all elements in the programmes of study for modern foreign languages at Key Stage 3. We would have to know more about Jamie's responses and achievements over time in order to assign any level to his responses with confidence. We would argue, however, that Jamie's experience has relevance both in terms of his individual priorities for learning and the curriculum.

Readers may have their own views about the relevance of the learning outcomes achieved by Jamie in terms of his IEP targets and the subject content of the lesson in which he has been involved. At the bottom of Figure 6.12 is a series of prompts to remind readers that these kinds of evaluative judgements about the significance of pupil responses should lead to:

■ revision or refinement of the targets in IEPs and, ultimately, of the long-term goals towards which pupils, parents and staff may be working;

■ review and development of short-term, medium-term and long-term curriculum plans, schemes of work and, ultimately, policy in relation to the subjects of the school curriculum;

- reports on the progress made by individual pupils, in relation to both the curriculum and their individual goals and targets, and consideration of the achievements of cohorts of pupils in relation to whole-school targets.

Records of experience based on curriculum planning documentation may be used to audit the breadth of the curriculum offered to pupils over time (see Chapters 8 and 9). Responses to individual learning needs may dictate variations in balance in the short term, medium term or long term (see Chapter 7) but individual target setting will ensure both progression through a pupil's school experiences over time and continuity of intent and approach across the curriculum. Individual targets thus lend coherence to learning opportunities that may otherwise become fragmented and inconsistent.

Closing comments

As we said at the start of this chapter, we do not believe that it is necessary for experienced teachers to undertake written short-term planning in detail for every lesson provided that medium-term curriculum plans and individual education planning procedures are suitably robust and effective. No purpose is served in having hard-pressed teachers copy out extracts from medium-term plans and IEPs in order to fill in boxes on short-term planning or lesson planning formats. This can often amount to empty bureaucracy and form filling for its own sake.

We do not suggest that short-term planning is unimportant, however. We simply propose that it is often internal and ephemeral. The checklist given as Table 6.1 may be used an an aide-memoire to remind staff of the important elements in the short-term planning process. We suggest that these elements are best thought of as planning and thinking processes rather than recording tasks. Individual schools and teachers may make their own decisions about which outcomes of which of these processes need to be committed to paper under which circumstances and for what purpose. The blank format given as Figure 6.13 will enable colleagues to debate these issues as a staff development activity; to audit their current practices; and to come to agreements about those aspects of short-term planning, considered in relation to medium-term plans and IEPs, that need to be committed to paper.

Table 6.1 Short-term planning checklist

Short-Term Planning should enable staff to …

- differentiate objectives from SCHEMES of WORK to promote access, participation and achievement for all learners

- integrate targets from INDIVIDUAL EDUCATION/LEARNING PLANS, set in terms of key cross-curricular skills, into curriculum-related group activities

(This should provide staff (and pupils/students) with clarity about BOTH curriculum-related learning opportunities AND ways of addressing priorities for individual pupils/students within the group.)

- detail ACTIVITIES which ALL learners will find challenging and accessible

(This should inform staff about what pupils/students, across a range of prior interests, aptitudes and achievements, are actually going to DO in lessons – with adaptations and extensions as appropriate.)

- negotiate, agree and communicate about the ROLES and RESPONSIBILITIES of different members of the teaching team deployed in support of pupil/student learning

(This should provide everyone – teacher/lecturer, support staff, paramedics, volunteers etc. – with clarity about expectations and ways to check what they should be doing.)

- select, organise and use a range of ENVIRONMENTS, RESOURCES and EQUIPMENT which is carefully matched to session content and priorities for individual pupils/students

(This should allow staff and pupils/students to prepare efficiently and effectively for each session of the day, providing for: changes of venue and equipment; and consistency of support where appropriate.)

- GROUP students in a variety of ways matched to a variety of purposes

(This should encompass teaching: to the whole class; to large cross-class groups; in homogenous 'sets'; in small mixed or 'jigsawed' groups; in pairs; or one-to-one etc.)

- develop balance and variety over time across a range of TEACHING METHODS and individual APPROACHES to LEARNING matched to lesson content and pupil/student preferences

(This should provide pupils/students with experience of, for example: active, investigative learning; watching and listening; problem-solving; collaboration with peers; independent work; using ICT etc.)

- create opportunities to RECORD and ASSESS pupils'/students' progress and achievement in relation to BOTH schemes of work AND individual education/learning plans

(This should provide staff and pupils/students with manageable amounts of good quality evidence to support the processes of monitoring student development; reviewing targets; planning future teaching and learning; reporting progress and achievement – and monitoring school/college development.)

… on a week-by-week, day-by-day, session-by-session basis.

Figure 6.13 Blank audit sheet for short-term planning

Short-Term Planning Checklist

Do your structures for short-term planning enable you to:

- differentiate objectives from SCHEMES of WORK

- integrate targets from INDIVIDUAL EDUCATION/LEARNING PLANS

- detail ACTIVITIES

- negotiate, agree and communicate about ROLES and RESPONSIBILITIES

- use a range of ENVIRONMENTS, RESOURCES and EQUIPMENT

- GROUP learners in a variety of ways

- develop balance and variety in approaches to TEACHING and LEARNING

- RECORD and ASSESS learners' progress and achievement

... on a week-by-week, day-by-day, lesson-by-lesson basis?

7 Meeting individual needs

Individual education planning

Earlier in this book, we described the development of differentiated schemes of work designed to meet the diverse needs of cohorts or groups of pupils. We focused on the process of development and emphasised that the opportunities to work and learn together presented to staff while they work on curriculum planning materials are more important, in our view, than any 'finished' or 'completed' paperwork. We would make precisely parallel comments about the development of individual education plans. While staff frequently express a great deal of concern about paper formats and procedural niceties related to the plan itself, there is often less professional interest in some of the key principles and practices that underpin the individual education planning process itself – a process we summarised in Table 1.2. We would like to open this chapter, therefore, with a review of those key principles.

As we have seen, the *Special Educational Needs Code of Practice* (DfES 2001a) is the item of guidance that most significantly informs provision in relation to individual pupils with special educational needs. According to the SEN Code, an IEP should be used to plan the interventions made for individual pupils through Early Years Action or Early Years Action Plus; School Action or School Action Plus; and through Statements of Special Educational Needs. In other words, an IEP should be developed for any pupil who, in order to achieve, requires structured interventions to be made that are additional to or different from the work planned for all pupils. This includes those pupils who are included in mainstream schools and those who receive their education in specialist settings.

The SEN Code states that the prime purpose of an IEP is to record strategies used to enable a pupil to progress. The first principle underpinning the development of IEPs is therefore that they should focus on positive developments, learning and achievement. Secondly, the SEN Code makes it clear that IEPs should focus on matters that are 'additional to or different from' the work that is provided for all pupils through the 'differentiated curriculum plan' or, in our terms, schemes of work. This means that where there is a well-differentiated scheme of work for science, let us say, in Key Stage 2, there will be no need to write further science targets into the IEPs of those pupils with special educational needs. As we shall see below, it is possible that additional or different work in science has been identified as a priority area of learning and development for a particular individual pupil (perhaps as a set of sensory experiences for a pupil with a visual or hearing impairment), in which case it may become appropriate to address this work through an IEP target. To pursue another example, it may also be important to take the differentiation of schemes of work a stage further by highlighting a particular cluster of literacy targets for a particular group of pupils experiencing difficulties in literacy, in which case it will be possible to develop a group education plan (GEP) focusing on this area of work for this group of pupils (DfES 2001b). The key principle here is that IEPs should focus on priority areas of learning for individual pupils with special educational needs rather than on repeating or refining objectives that are already set out in schemes of work designed to meet the needs of all pupils.

In this way, as schools become more inclusive and staff become more skilled at differentiating schemes of work in order to make them relevant and available to learners with special educational needs, we anticipate that there will be less need for IEPs, particularly those that address targets in core curriculum areas. The SEN Code itself makes it clear that IEPs should be brief and highly focused, containing, in total, just 'three or four individual targets' designed to 'match the child's needs' and most probably addressing key areas of learning and development including communication, literacy, number work, behaviour or social skills. It follows that there is no need for any particular IEP to address all these areas. Targets in IEPs should address issues that are priorities for individual pupils. Where one pupil's IEP may therefore contain two communication targets and a behaviour target, the IEP for another pupil may address three priorities in relation to personal and social development and a numeracy target.

The SEN Code suggests that the targets in IEPs should be 'short-term'. We interpret this to indicate time-spans measured in weeks rather than months or years. Indeed, the SEN Code itself states that targets should be reviewed 'at least twice a year' but ideally each term or even more frequently in acute or fast-moving circumstances. We suggest that IEP targets might routinely be set for half a term while acknowledging that, for some pupils in some areas, it is difficult to break targets down into time-frames of less than a term.

What should be in an IEP?

According to the *SEN Code of Practice* and the associated *Toolkit* (DfES 2001a, 2001b), the IEP should be focused on enabling a pupil with special educational needs to make progress in areas of learning that are of direct relevance to the individual. The IEP format should include information about:

- short-term targets for learning set for, with or by the pupil
- teaching strategies that can be used to address the targets
- any special provision that is to be put in place to support learning
- the date at which the IEP will be reviewed
- success criteria that will enable staff and pupils to make judgements about when the targets have been met
- the outcomes achieved by the pupil, which will be recorded formally when the IEP is reviewed.

Figures 7.1 to 7.3 provide examples of IEP formats in use in schools known to us. In Figure 7.1, which is an extract from the IEP paperwork used in Reuben's school, staff have set out the aims discussed at annual review and the short-term targets derived from them. For Reuben, in this particular term, these focus upon priority areas in terms of personal and social development and skills in health, hygiene and safety. In order to support assessment of Reuben's progress towards his short-term targets, staff have also set out, for each target, illustrative examples of possible evidence of success. These suggest the sorts of choice-making, interactive and self-help behaviours that Reuben may realistically demonstrate this term in view of his prior achievements and the group activities he will encounter. In cases where more detail is required about the

Figure 7.1 Reuben's individual education plan

Section 2
Reuben's
Key targets

This section records the aims set in terms of key cross-curricular skills for the coming year; the short-term targets derived from them; and possible evidence of success (how we know if targets are achieved). The strategies and approaches to be used to teach and support the achievement of the targets will include: one-to-one teaching, paired work, small group work, whole-class teaching, verbal and visual prompts, shadowing and peer coaching. If other, more specific strategies are used (yes ○ no ○) see section 2a.

XCS	Component skill	Aims from Statement	Short-term targets	Possible evidence of success
PSH	Personal	To develop his ability to make and express choices.	To make choices with understanding in a variety of contexts.	Pointing to choice of juice and spread at snack time, dessert at lunch-time. Selecting an instrument from a box containing a number of instruments. Moving towards sand play or colouring table when given a choice of activity. Choosing whether to have drink or biscuit, first by pointing to photograph.
	Social	To develop his social skills.	To develop a greater awareness of his peers, beginning to interact with them during paired and small group work.	Rolling a ball or pushing a car back and forth in simple turn-taking play. Passing a hat to named person in a small group. Holding hands with peer during music and movement activities.
	Health, Hygiene and Safety	To develop his independence in self-help and personal care skills.	To actively assist in aspects of familiar self-care routines including feeding and dressing skills.	Routinely digging and bringing a loaded spoon to his mouth, feeding himself cut-up food using a sloping dish and dycem mat. Drinking independently from an open cup, replacing on table between sips. Feeding self a variety of finger foods, maintaining grip on biscuits between bites. Removing top clothing items once he has been helped to do most of it. Pulling garments such as socks off.
Key				

PSH: Personal, Social and Health Skills; **C:** Communication skills; **M:** Mathematics skills; **P:** Physical skills
PS: Problem solving skills; **ICT:** Information and communication technology skills; **SS:** Study skills

Figure 7.2 Meena's individual education plan

Meena – Targets for summer term, as identified at annual review

	COMMUNICATION	IMPROVING OWN LEARNING	WORKING WITH OTHERS
AIM	To pass information to a large group of familiar adults	To increase confidence when speaking in front of a familiar group	To increase confidence when interacting with other children
BASELINE	Meena is keen to pass on information to familiar adults whom she sees most days. She is also quite chatty with other adults whom she sees regularly, particularly in the secure and familiar environment of the classroom.	Meena is now more confident when speaking in front of a group in familiar and repetitive routines within the class environment. She is also beginning to offer one-word answers to simple questions in the class group.	Meena is generally more aware of others when playing and is beginning to use suggestions to involve them in her play. She will often rely on the involvement of adults to involve or interact with others, often looking to them for support.
SPECIFIC OBJECTIVE	To pass on simple messages to a familiar adult outside the classroom. Each time on five consecutive occasions.	To give a short verbal response when working as part of familiar class group. Each time on five consecutive occasions.	To lead playmate in 'follow the leader' activity. Each time on three consecutive occasions.
STRATEGIES	Adult to give Meena simple messages to convey to familiar member of staff. Clear and simple language to use: two words, if Meena chooses to use these. Accompany this with picture, symbolic or written clue and involve another child if necessary so Meena not alone. Initially adult to accompany Meena.	With range of questions, choice of two words or opportunity to fill in words in sentence, give Meena opportunity and time to give verbal response when working as part of whole-class group. Praise 'good talking' and also indicate if Meena uses a strong voice when speaking at these times.	Adult encourage other child to copy Meena's movement on playground or in soft play environment initially. Draw Meena's attention to the child copying her. Praise any original ideas, acknowledgement of other child and any interaction with them. Give opportunity for Meena to initiate activity.
RESOURCES	Staff Familiar adult Prompt card	Staff Whole-class settings	Staff Other children School environment
MONITORING	Errand General level of confidence Support necessary	General level of confidence Support necessary	Context Prompt necessary Acknowledgement of others

Figure 7.3 Review of Meena's individual education plan

Meena's progress at the end of the summer term

	COMMUNICATION	IMPROVING OWN LEARNING	WORKING WITH OTHERS
REVIEW OF PROGRESS	Meena has made good progress with this objective and is generally demonstrating a greater degree of confidence. Meena has passed on a number of messages and has made herself clear and understood on a few occasions. She has taken messages to familiar class staff in other situations and to office staff. On most occasions Meena will now make an audible single-word request, although is not always understood. At these times Meena will repeat herself with some encouragement and is usually happy to approach a small number of familiar staff.	Meena has again made really good progress and has achieved this objective within her familiar class. She is demonstrating a greater confidence, particularly when filling in words and answering questions in the group literacy session. Meena has responded well to the clear expectations and is also showing a good understanding when familiar adults share their expectations of her verbal contribution. Meena responds well to praise from an adult and is beginning to respond to a glance when more is expected.	Meena has responded well to these activities both at school and particularly when on her integration placement. She enjoys leading the others who copy her actions and although she rarely uses verbal interaction at this time, appears very confident in her movements. At these times Meena responds very well to the praise given by an adult.
FURTHER DEVELOPMENT	Continue above looking for consistency. To pass on simple message to familiar adult outside the classroom. Each time on five consecutive occasions.	Initially continue above to establish in new class group. To give a short verbal response when working as part of familiar class group. Each time on five consecutive occasions.	Extend to include verbal interaction. To continue verbal turn-taking game. On three consecutive occasions.
DATE ACHIEVED			
DATE CHECKED			

precise strategies to be used to teach a particular skill, staff will note these in a further section of the IEP.

In Figure 7.2, an example from another school, staff give aims in the three key areas of communication, improving own learning and working with others established at Meena's annual review. A sense of the baseline from which Meena will hopefully be making progress is given together with a set of short-term objectives, with a sense of the success criteria seen as realistic and appropriate in Meena's case. Examples of the strategies to be used to teach these skills, again located firmly in the day-to-day flow of group activity in the classroom and the school in general, are given together with some notes about any resources that may be particularly useful. Staff are prompted to look out for opportunities to monitor and assess progress. In Figure 7.3, we provide the records made in relation to Meena's IEP targets at the end of one term. It is clear that Meena is making progress in these areas. In two cases, the sheet records a decision to continue working on the targets, either in order to achieve more consistency of response, as in the case of Meena's communication target, or in order to practise and consolidate an emerging skill in new contexts, as in the case of the target for improving Meena's own learning. Meena has been so successful in working towards her target for working with others that this target will be extended to take in new forms of verbal interaction – progress that will relate closely to her developing communication skills. Meena's IEP format incorporates boxes in which achievements and checked achievements can be noted and dated.

Individual support programmes

In order for the IEP itself to provide a 'graduated response to special educational needs' and to remain 'crisply written' and focused on a small selection of three or four priority targets for learning, it is important that IEPs are not used to set out ongoing strategies for the management of medical, paramedical or behavioural issues. The IEP should remain focused on progress made in learning in the short term and its prime function is to inform staff and pupils about targets for that learning. While it may be appropriate to include in an IEP, for example, short-term targets designed to help pupils to learn to manage their own behaviour or their own medical or paramedical procedures (see below), IEPs should not be used to set out support or management protocols to be followed by staff. As confirmed by QCA/DfEE (2001a), these matters can be set out separately in individual support programmes to inform and remind staff about agreed approaches to providing support for pupils':

- mobility and positioning
- communication
- sensory difficulties
- personal care, hygiene and use of the toilet
- eating, drinking and nutrition
- medical, paramedical or therapeutic regimes
- emotional and behavioural difficulties.

The information given in individual support programmes will be addressed to the staff responsible for providing ongoing support in these areas. The programme will therefore describe staff roles and responsibilities in managing these issues rather than targets for pupil learning. The contents of each individual support programme should, of course, be subjected to review at least annually. However, it is likely that these programmes will remain relevant in the long to medium term since they will be designed to support pupils experiencing persistent difficulties and the ongoing implications of sensory or physical impairments. Figures 7.4 to 7.7 provide examples of formats for individual support programming. In Figure 7.4, a support profile of Lewis, a pupil with severe learning difficulties and some behavioural difficulties, offers staff working with him in an inclusive setting some basic information about him and his needs and preferences. Figure 7.5 provides a format for a behaviour management programme, detailing, for an individual learner, up to four problematic behaviours and the agreed staff responses that will be used in each case.

Figure 7.6 gives a format, devised in a specialist setting, for setting out protocols for supporting eating and drinking for individuals with profound and complex learning difficulties. Details will be entered into this format by school staff, therapists and parents working collaboratively and used to ensure that mealtime routines for each young person are consistent, safe and comfortable for the learner whoever is providing meal-time support. Space allows a reminder about any self-help targets written into the current IEP to be included in this format. This will ensure that even relatively long-term management protocols can remain focused on progress towards independence. Figure 7.7 provides opportunities to generate a similarly detailed account of the support needs of pupils with sensory and physical impairments, again with space for a note of any relevant IEP targets and to record a pupil's likes and dislikes. These sorts of formats will be crucial in ensuring that good quality information is used by all the people coming into contact with pupils with complex needs, including subject teachers, support staff and staff facilitating mealtimes and breaks.

The role of the key skills and other priorities for learning

As we suggested in Chapter 2, staff may decide to address certain aspects of the key skills framework through group activities planned, like other aspects of the curriculum, in differentiated schemes of work and implemented through dedicated timetabled sessions aimed at cohorts of pupils and students in particular age groups. It is possible, for example, that daily living skills may be taught in this way, particularly as students grow older and the need to engage with the preparation for adult life becomes a priority. These skills may include:

- domestic skills such as:
  - preparing food and managing a domestic budget
  - planning balanced meals and diets
  - cooking and using a range of kitchen appliances safely
- community skills such as:
  - going shopping
  - using public transport
  - learning about and using a range of facilities in the community
- leisure and recreational skills such as:
  - planning leisure activities and holidays
  - using recreational amenities in a local area
  - participating in the activities of a range of clubs, societies and organisations.

Staff may decide that the most effective way of promoting these skills will be through organised group activities planned as part of the curriculum for personal and social development (see, for example, Otten 1999). Staff working with pupils in younger age groups have also developed useful group approaches to the teaching of sensory

Figure 7.4 Lewis's pupil support profile

Name: Lewis   **Year:** 7   **Form:** 7B

Date set: September

To be reviewed: End of autumn term

Student profile

Lewis is a student with severe learning difficulties. He has verbal communication, which is limited, and he needs time to process information. He responds very well to positive praise and encouragement. He seeks physical attention, kisses, hugs and will attempt to sit on an adult's lap. Lewis will swear, shout and display inappropriate body language if attention is not shown to him or if he is unsure of a situation. Lewis will also scratch, pinch, bite, slap and kick if distressed. Rarely this will escalate, and he will become very violent and upset. He enjoys listening to music and time in the multi-sensory room. He is not yet familiar with sitting for more than ten minutes at a tabletop activity.

Details of student's intimate care needs

Toileting

Lewis is able to use the toilet with minimum assistance.

- Lewis will ask and sign to use the toilet.
- He must be accompanied to the toilet.
- He will ask for help to do his belt, buttons etc. – wait to be asked.
- Almost close the toilet door, to give Lewis privacy, remind him you are still there.
- Remind him to wipe, flush and wash his hands.

Feeding

Lewis is able to feed himself with minimum assistance.

- He needs help to collect his dinner and to carry his tray.
- Sit with Lewis, he may need help to cut his food up.
- He will, if left, grab at other people's food.
- Make sure he does not put too much food in his mouth.
- Assist him to take his tray to the counter.

Washing

Lewis is able to wash himself with minimum assistance.

- Give Lewis verbal prompts to wash himself, e.g. wash your mouth, wash your hands etc.

Dressing

Lewis is able to dress himself with minimum assistance.

- Give Lewis verbal prompts to dress himself, e.g. pull your arms out, over your head etc.

Equipment to be used

No special equipment to be used with Lewis.

It is very important to remember that every student should be given maximum privacy and should be encouraged to be as independent as possible at all times. Communicate to the child throughout assisting them, detailing what you are going to do and how, using communication that the child is familiar with. Always wear gloves if appropriate and use the correct equipment. If you are unsure about anything in this profile, contact:

Figure 7.5 Individual behaviour management programme

Name: **Year:**   **Form:**

Date set: **To be reviewed:**

Student profile

Behaviour characteristics and the agreed response to be taken

1.

Characteristic
Response

2.

Characteristic
Response

3.

Characteristic
Response

4.

Characteristic
Response

If you have any questions or concerns about this programme, please contact:

---

awareness and perception, involving the use and co-ordination of all available senses (see, for example, Pagliano 1999; Davis 2001); early thinking skills (see, for example, Jelly, Fuller and Byers 2000; Costello 2000; Wallace 2001) and, of course, key skills including communication (for example, Latham and Miles 2001) and the application of number (Berger, Morris and Portman 2000). Under these circumstances we suggest that these aspects of the curriculum can be addressed using plans and approaches like those described in Chapters 4, 5 and 6 of this book.

At other times, however, staff, pupils and parents will feel that it is more appropriate to address these and other skills through individual approaches. The skills that are likely to need to be addressed individually and that may constitute priority areas of learning for pupils with a range of special educational needs include:

- highly individualised approaches to communication, perhaps involving subtleties of facial expression or body language; the use of assistive technology; systems involving real objects, photographs, pictures and symbols; or signing;

- application of practical number skills in everyday community settings relevant to life outside and beyond school;

- use of information and communication technology in support of sensory development, communication, mobility, environmental control, independence and the completion and presentation of work in school and beyond;

- learning to take turns, share time and attention, co-operate, interact, socialise and work with others, including members of staff and peers;

Figure 7.6 Individual support programme

MEAL-TIME ROUTINE	
Name:	Date:
Utensils:	
Food:	
Dominant hand:	
Seating position:	
Helper's position:	
Routine:	
Drinks:	
Likes:	
Dislikes:	
Current objectives:	
Additional Notes:	

Figure 7.7 Individual support programme

NAME: SCHOOL YEAR: STAFFING:	SUPPORT NEEDS AND WAYS TO MINIMISE THE IMPACT OF:
SENSORY IMPAIRMENTS	PHYSICAL IMPAIRMENTS
MEDICAL and PARAMEDICAL ISSUES	PERSONAL CARE ROUTINES
RESOURCES and EQUIPMENT	SHORT-TERM PRIORITIES
LIKES and DISLIKES	OTHER NOTES

- becoming more self-aware, independent, motivated and self-managing as a learner, focusing attention on relevant tasks, working to completion, addressing and overcoming difficulties, recognising preferences, strengths and limitations and setting targets for future achievements;

- problem-solving and thinking skills, ranging from an understanding of cause and effect and skills in anticipation and prediction through to participation in group activity focused on the creative, imaginative and collaborative resolution of challenges;

- developing sensory awareness and perception, particularly for those pupils who have sensory impairments and who need to learn to make the most effective and co-ordinated use possible of their available senses, including vision, hearing, taste, touch and smell;

- skills in physical orientation and mobility, including positioning skills, fine and whole body movement and co-ordination, independent mobility and the use of aids;

- issues in personal care, including dressing and undressing, eating and drinking, use of the toilet and personal hygiene, and the management of medical and paramedical procedures;

- daily living skills, encompassing independent and interdependent use and maintenance of the home environment, safe and healthy living, food preparation, use of community facilities, and enjoyment of opportunities for leisure and recreation;

- the self-management of behaviour, including social behaviour and behaviour that challenges staff because it is self-injurious, confrontational or destructive or because it results in states of withdrawal and isolation;

- the management of emotions, arising from change, loss, frustration, anxiety and challenge or from periods of transition, such as adolescence, or low self-esteem.

These and other related issues are dealt with in more depth in *Developing Skills* (QCA/DfEE 2001b). We suggest that staff in schools will also wish to take forward their own thinking in relation to these areas of learning. This will enable them to develop highly individualised approaches to setting targets, teaching skills, and recording and reviewing progress through IEPs focused on priorities for learning that are specific to each pupil with special educational needs. As we have emphasised above, we are not proposing that any single IEP would address all these areas at once. While many potential areas for development may be discussed and noted at annual review meetings and in other discussions with parents, pupils and professionals, school staff will need to focus each IEP on a manageable selection of focused short-term targets. The notes provided in Table 7.1 will help staff to develop their practice in relation to IEP targets. We suggest that the negotiation and refinement of areas to address in IEPs, and discussion of the influence of IEP targets on other areas of learning, should be undertaken in collaboration between school staff, including teachers and support staff, other professionals, parents and the pupils themselves.

Breadth and balance

Individual target setting may mean that balance in the curriculum changes for a particular pupil over a given period of time. Staff, in consultation with the pupil, the parents and often other professionals, may deliberately create short-term imbalance in order to address specific issues of relevance and priority. For instance:

- a pupil with English as a second home language may benefit from a finite period of immersion in language activity;
- a pupil recovering from corrective surgery may require an intensive programme of frequent, regular physiotherapy;
- a recently bereaved pupil may need to spend time experiencing the support of a counselling relationship in place of regular lessons.

Each of these examples of temporary curricular enrichment is consistent with the definition of the whole curriculum that we explored in Chapter 2. The task for staff is to ensure that pupils receive an entitlement to breadth over time, even where balance is variable in the short term.

In the same way, learning priorities for pupils with particular needs may dictate an emphasis on certain areas of the curriculum in the longer term. For example:

- achieving an appropriate position prior to engaging in curriculum-related activity is likely to demand significant amounts of time and staff support for a pupil with cerebral palsy;
- time devoted to multi-sensory, tactile and olfactory experiences is likely to be of long-term benefit to a pupil who is isolated from peers, from staff, and from the visual and aural environment by sensory impairments;
- regular individual sessions of music therapy may help to maintain a pupil with social and communicative difficulties in integrated class groupings for most of the time.

Again, these variations in conventional balance are consistent with definitions of the whole curriculum (NCC 1990, 1992; SCAA 1995); with the function of the National Curriculum as a framework for developing breadth and balance in the school curriculum (DfEE/QCA 1999a, 1999b; QCA/DfES 2001a); and with the need to secure relevance in the curriculum for individual pupils (DfES 2001a).

Decisions about individual education planning and curriculum balance should not be taken by teaching staff only. To achieve a real focus on individual priorities and the development of the whole pupil, the views of a range of professionals (including,

Table 7.1 Are your IEP targets SMART?

Specific

Are the targets specific to this particular pupil?
Are they linked to her/his Statement and annual review?
Do they address 'extra' or 'additional' priorities and avoid unnecessary duplication of objectives already specified in schemes of work?

Measurable

Do the targets address particular skills or accomplishments?
Do they specify proposed levels of prompting or support?

Are they set in terms of well-defined, observable outcomes so that:

- You are looking for significant, new responses?
- Everyone knows what to record and when?
- Staff will know when the target is achieved?
- The pupil will know when the target is achieved?

Achievable

Is the progress implied by the targets realistic:

- for this pupil?
- in this time-frame?
- with these levels of resourcing?

Should the targets be broken down into smaller steps?

Relevant

Do the targets address the priority areas of learning for this pupil?
Are they designed to meet real needs in the whole curriculum?
Is there a small number of tightly focused targets?
Will everyone involved understand the circumstances or context in which the target can be addressed?

Time-limited

When is the agreed point of short-term review for these targets?
Should the timescale be more tightly focused?
If the target is achieved within the timescale, what next?

It is worth noting that some targets may involve:

- experimentation and exploration in new areas of learning;
- consolidation, maintenance, transfer, generalisation of pre-existing skills, knowledge, understanding etc;
- slowing or reduction in rates of regression.

A 'method' section aligned to targets should be used to detail the circumstances or contexts in which the targets can be addressed – activities, resources, equipment, staff roles, pupil groupings, rewards etc.
Individual support programmes can be used to give information about consistent approaches to the management of physical positioning, mobility, aided and augmented communication, problematic behaviour, sensory impairments, personal care regimes, medical and paramedical issues, therapies and therapeutic approaches, counselling etc.

for example, support staff, teaching assistants and therapists) as well as parents and/or carers and the pupils themselves and/or their advocates should be taken into account. Indeed, the SEN Code states unequivocally that 'the IEP should be discussed with the child and the parents' and that the IEP targets themselves may be set 'by the child'. Pupils and parents, as we shall see below, should be involved not only in setting targets but also in monitoring progress and in the regular review of the IEP itself. The SEN Code proposes that at least one review in the year should be scheduled in order to give parents a chance to express their views and that, 'wherever possible, the child should also take part in the review process'. Where this close and direct level of involvement proves problematic (for example, for a pupil with profound communication difficulties), the pupil's 'ascertainable views' should be taken into account. The following paragraphs look in more detail at the issue of pupil involvement.

Setting targets – pupil involvement

The revised *SEN Code of Practice* (DfES 2001a) places renewed emphasis upon involving pupils in setting their own learning targets. This reinforces principles established in other documents and legislation such as the *Convention on the Rights of the Child* (United Nations 1989) and the Children Act (DoH 1989). The value of involving pupils in the management of their own learning has been well established (Griffiths and Davies 1995; Davie and Galloway 1996; Davie, Upton and Varma 1996). Preparation for an adult life where individuals are regularly called upon to make decisions must be an important consideration in all schools. The involvement of pupils in making decisions about their own learning can play an important role in enabling them to increase independence, understand their own learning needs, and learn important skills such as negotiation and choice making. Munby (1995) suggests that those pupils who are involved in such processes become more accurate in understanding their own abilities and performance, while Cooper (1993), Bennathan (1996) and Marland (1996) provide clear indications of how the involvement of pupils in target setting and decisions about their own needs can lead to improved behaviour.

In many schools the provision of opportunities to enable pupils to make decisions has been a feature of the later years of schooling. However, for pupils with special educational needs it is appropriate to consider how pupils may play a greater role even from the earliest years of their school lives. This may begin with simple choice making, possibly at break-times or in relation to choosing which book they would like to take to read at home, but can also involve pupils in discussions about their own progress, personal learning strengths and preferences. Pupils can be encouraged to discuss their own learning needs and to set targets almost as soon as they begin school.

Staff at some infant schools involve pupils in the identification of their own learning strengths and needs from the time when they first enter school. Staff report that this encourages greater independence and enables pupils to take some responsibility for monitoring their own learning. Figure 7.8 gives an example of a self-recording sheet, related to individual targets, designed for use in Key Stage 1. The sheet enables pupils to put stamps or stickers, indicating 'need more practice', 'OK' or 'achieved', into recording boxes each time they attempt an activity related to their target. This level of involvement requires careful management on the part of the teacher, who will need to have a good knowledge of individual pupils in order to be able to use approaches that promote understanding and help pupils to address personal targets that are appropriate to individual needs.

Potential barriers to involvement in target setting

The involvement of pupils with special educational needs in target setting presents staff with a number of further challenges. Some of these may be the result of difficulties in the areas of language and communication and may require staff to develop materials that use symbols or other forms of augmentative communication. A further barrier to progress may exist where pupils have never been encouraged to become independent and have always had decisions made for them.

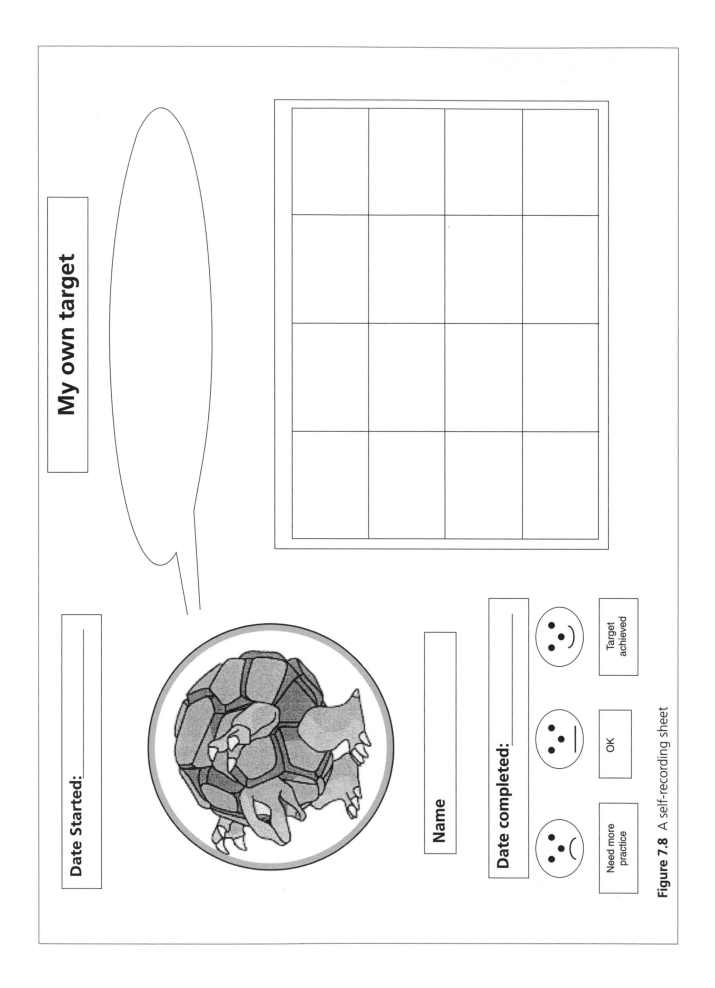

My own target

Date Started: _____

Name _____

Date completed: _____

Need more practice   OK   Target achieved

Figure 7.8 A self-recording sheet

Staff who have engaged in target-setting processes with pupils with special educational needs have identified a number of potential obstacles which need to be considered when developing policy and practice in this area. These potential obstacles, which should be reviewed in relation to individual pupils and will need to be addressed in the light of their individual needs, prior achievements and aptitudes, include:

- **Suggestibility:** Some pupils with learning difficulties have become used to complying with adult requests and following instructions. Indeed, many pupils will have been taught to behave in these compliant ways. Such pupils will appear to be 'eager to please' and can be easily led into making decisions which they have not thought out for themselves.

- **Communication:** Some pupils experience difficulties in communicating through conventional means and the use of augmentative systems of communication, including symbols, photographs, objects of reference or tactile cues (Fergusson 1994), may be required to support their involvement in target setting.

- **Dependency:** Pupils who have never been encouraged to make independent decisions may take a long time and need a great deal of careful support if they are to break away from dependency upon adults.

- **Timing:** Some schools do not begin to involve pupils in target setting until the later years of their education. This can result in difficulties in breaking established dependencies and insufficient time being available to develop the essential competencies.

- **Lack of component skills:** The goals of independent decision-making and becoming an effective target setter are dependent upon the acquisition of a range of specific skills. These should not be assumed and are likely to need to be taught.

Overcoming barriers to involvement

Some staff working in special schools for pupils with severe and profound and multiple learning difficulties have developed assessment schedules related to the skills and understanding which pupils need in order to become effective target setters and decision-makers. Figures 7.9 to 7.11 provide examples of sheets used to assess the progress made by pupils in developing skills as target setters and decision-makers. These approaches often entail providing a proforma which staff complete and revisit on a regular basis. By using this schedule, they are able to identify pupil strengths and weaknesses and incorporate approaches that address pupil needs within their lessons. Staff regularly reassess their pupils and ensure that, when they are planning lessons, they take account of opportunities to develop skills such as negotiation or prediction which are critical features of effective decision-making. Research undertaken into the work of one of these schools, with a particular focus upon pupil involvement in target setting, has shown that pupils with severe learning difficulties can make progress in developing independence and decision-making through careful planning of the target-setting process (Rose, Fletcher and Goodwin 1999; Rose 1999; Fletcher 2001).

A number of principles for involving pupils in the target-setting process can be identified from this work. These include:

- Involve pupils in choice and decision-making from the earliest stages of schooling.

- Discuss pupils' targets with them regularly in order to keep these at the forefront of their attention.

- Ensure that pupils are aware of how they are doing in making progress towards the achievement of targets. Visual representations such as progress charts can help.

Figure 7.9 Pupil involvement assessment: knowledge/recognition of potential

	Yes/No	Comment	Next Step?
1. Recognition/identification of achievements	☐		
2. Knowing when something has been achieved	☐		
3. Identifying personal strengths and weaknesses	☐		
4. Identifying likes and dislikes	☐		
5. Identifying possible future leaving (post-school) needs	☐		
6. Recognition of having had an effect upon decisions	☐		
7. Identification of something which cannot be achieved	☐		
8. Recognition of something which cannot be done yet, but which can be achieved	☐		
9. Identification of possible learning strategies, including support required	☐		
10. Recognition of something which the target setter could not do, but can do now	☐		
11. Acknowledgement and identification of difficulties or non-achievement experienced	☐		
12. Understanding of concepts of hard, easy and manageable	☐		

■ Find the most appropriate means of communicating with individual pupils and use these approaches consistently.

■ Avoid involving pupils in too many targets – in some cases a single target may be appropriate.

In some instances, adults will need to act as advocates on behalf of the child. This requires careful consideration in order to ensure that pupils' rights are protected and that appropriate relationships between professionals and parents are maintained. Where statements about pupils' abilities, needs or wishes are to be made and recorded as if they are the pupil's own, it is essential that advocates are able to provide evidence to support the views being expressed. It is equally important that the role of the advocate, in representing the views of the pupil, is clearly articulated to all interested parties. There may be times when the targets set in collaboration with the pupil may not be seen as having the same degree of importance as those targets set with a parent or carer or by another professional 'colleague'. Clear policy on pupil involvement is essential in order to ensure that the purpose of such actions is understood and that it is consistently managed throughout the school.

Fletcher (2001) has provided examples of the importance that the pupils themselves, as well as members of staff, attach to involvement in target setting. He has also

Figure 7.10 Pupil involvement assessment: negotiation

	Yes/No	Comment	Next Step?
1. Can state an opinion with confidence.			
2. Can disagree with confidence.			
3. Takes part in a two-way conversation.			
4. Can say 'yes' and 'no' in response to requests.			
5. Seeks clarification and help when unable to understand.			
6. Expresses personal feelings and needs.			
7. Maintains and develops a topic of conversation effectively and appropriately.			
8. Stands up for self – can represent own views and feelings in an assertive and non-aggressive way.			
9. Makes suggestions and gives opinions in the correct context.			
10. Has well-developed skills of refusal which are used effectively and appropriately, i.e. ability to oppose something he or she does not agree with and to use appropriate verbal or non-verbal skills to reinforce refusal.			
11. Achieves a good balance between listening and responding.			
12. Is able to initiate conversations successfully.			
13. Adapts behaviour and language to the context and listener.			

Figure 7.11 Pupil involvement assessment: prediction skills – concept of time

	Yes/No	Comment	Next Step?
1. Understands the concept of time in relation to the target set.			
2. Understands differences in timescales – day/week/term etc.			
3. Identifies/recognises/states the benefits of achieving a target.			

noted that involving pupils in target setting is a time-consuming process which demands careful planning and a clarity of intent on the part of all staff in schools. However, those schools that invest time in the development of effective target-setting systems are likely to find that pupils gain considerably in their independence and ability to make informed decisions. The next chapter of this book includes some discussion of how these gains can be consolidated when pupils are also involved in the processes of record keeping, assessment and reporting.

Issues in assessment, recording and reporting

The processes involved in assessment, recording and reporting have received considerable attention in most schools. Yet these processes still create difficulties which mean that schools struggle to develop assessment, recording and reporting formats that are informative and manageable while adequately meeting the needs of all pupils and members of staff. In some schools, it is still possible to find a wide range of approaches being used and, while many of these may be effective in their own right, a lack of consistency across a school has a detrimental effect upon planning and curriculum delivery. Chesworth (1994) demonstrated the value of in-school collaboration in the development of a co-ordinated response to record keeping. As she rightly states, the relationship between assessment, recording, and reporting and all other aspects of the curriculum is a complex one and, for this reason, concentration upon any of these in isolation from the whole process of curriculum development is likely to lead to difficulties and frustrations. In this book, we have tried to illustrate, through examples, some of the opportunities that exist for incorporating assessment, recording and reporting at all stages of the curriculum development process. In this chapter we will consider some of the relationships that exist between these important elements and other aspects of the curriculum.

Recognising opportunities at the planning stage

In this book, we emphasise the importance of involving pupils at all stages of the education process, including planning, recording, assessment and reporting. Research suggests that few schools have made significant progress in meeting these requirements in all areas (MacNamara and Rose 1995). While some have made moves towards pupil involvement in evaluation of their own learning, the number of schools involving them at the planning stage is still relatively small. Hardwick and Rushton (1994) describe the potential that exists for greater involvement of pupils with special needs in action planning, a process which they see as critical in developing pupils' skills of communication, negotiation and understanding of intended learning outcomes. Galton (1989) also emphasises the importance of the pupil/teacher dialogue, during which agreed standards for performance can be reached and mutual criteria for assessment established. Pupils involved at the planning stage (see Chapter 7) have a clearer view of teacher expectations; can be assisted in identifying areas of work that may cause them difficulties; and have an opportunity to feel valued in the whole learning process.

Clarity of intention is an important feature of good teaching. The pupil who has an understanding of teacher expectations, and has shared in the planning process, feels valued and has an increased incentive to perform well. Action planning and the sharing of objectives require a positive relationship between the teacher and the pupil. A partnership based upon trust and respect must be established but this process can, in itself, be an important element in influencing the development of a positive attitude to learning. Establishing this approach need not be a complicated procedure, but the provision of some form of agreement between teacher and pupil is necessary if it is to operate smoothly.

Figures 8.1 and 8.2 provide simple examples of how teacher planning and student/pupil input can be combined. These sheets offer pupils opportunities to comment upon their priorities within given subjects, while teachers also declare their objectives for learning. In addition to the statement about planning, the same sheets contain an area for reporting upon progress. This is followed by a box to be used for an agreed statement which can be signed by both the teacher and the student.

Such approaches are being developed in many schools, including those for pupils with severe learning difficulties (Lawson 1992; Hardwick and Rushton 1994). Symbol systems, or other forms of augmented communication, have been used to good effect in enabling pupils with learning or communication difficulties to gain access to action planning. Fergusson (1994) has indicated the importance of seeing such approaches as part of a continuum which, while providing an end in themselves for some pupils, will be seen as a step towards more complex forms of communication for many. Pupils who do not use traditional orthography should not be denied access to joint planning. Many teachers who have become proficient in the use of photography, video and information technology for recording progress and experience are now using the same media to support pupil involvement in planning. This, at the simplest level, may begin with the use of symbols, pictures or photographs on personal timetables and may be followed by lesson planning sheets that include lesson content and intended outcomes.

The planning stage is critical for the effective monitoring of learning outcomes (see Chapter 5). Plans should, of course, relate directly to school policy, to schemes of work and to individual education programmes (as we suggest in the relevant chapters in this book). The planning stage may equally serve as a guideline during the curriculum monitoring process when the subject co-ordinator is attempting to make observations concerning breadth and balance (see Chapter 9).

Assessment in action

Throughout this book we have emphasised the place of assessment as an integral part of the teaching process, built into the curriculum and not added on at a later stage. Assessment is largely about the collection of evidence related to what has been taught and what pupils have learned. As such, it should inform teachers and enable them to plan more effectively. Assessment is not synonymous with testing and, while tests may have a place in the assessment of pupils, they should not be used exclusively to make judgements about pupil progress. Assessment should relate directly to pupil needs and to teaching. Rouse (1991) has described the way in which testing can become almost ritualistic in some schools and education authorities, conducted on a regular basis to provide statistics which have little direct bearing upon what happens in the classroom. Educational 'league tables', which supply charts of figures and encourage generalised statements about and invidious comparisons between the performances of schools, have little intrinsic value in a system that aims to support teachers in addressing the needs of a diverse population. Of far greater value to

Figure 8.1 Teacher planning and recording sheet

TEACHER PLANNING AND RECORDING SHEET
(To be completed in conjunction with the student sheet)

STUDENT'S NAME   **SUBJECT**   **TERM**

This term in   the course will be:

                    has identified the following areas for improvement:

He/she also needs to consider:

This term   did well in the following areas:

The following areas need more work during next term:

AGREED STATEMENT

This report has been shared with student, and his/her report has also been shared.
The following statement has been agreed by both the student and teacher.

Figure 8.2 Student planning and recording sheet

STUDENT PLANNING AND RECORDING SHEET	NAME
SUBJECT	TERM

This term in   I will be doing:

The things I would like to do better at are:

The things which I enjoyed this term were:

The things which were not quite so good were:

I think I have improved at:

I still need to do better at:

schools, and to the pupils within them, is a system that values assessment as a means of identifying the progress pupils make and assists in the planning of routes for further development.

In the revised National Curriculum (DfEE/QCA 1999a, 1999b), significant moves have been made towards placing an emphasis upon classroom-based assessment procedures as opposed to standardised tests, thus recognising the value of teacher assessment and the integrity of the profession in monitoring the learning of all pupils. This process has been taken forward with the introduction of the 'P scales' (DfEE/QCA 1998, revised 2001; QCA/DfEE 2001a). These 'differentiated performance criteria' outline learning and attainment below Level 1 in all the National Curriculum subjects, including citizenship, religious education and PSHE. Levels P4 to P8 begin to describe learning that is subject-specific and that leads smoothly into attainment in relation to each subject at Level 1 and beyond. Levels P1 to P3 concern learning that is less easily differentiated by subject, although subject-focused examples of responses are given in the QCA/DfEE materials. Achievements at these early levels encompass a continuum of responses from tolerance of an experience (an 'encounter'); through the beginnings of awareness and response; towards more focused and active engagement, participation and involvement. Although they are intended for use in both mainstream and specialist contexts, the P scales are thus designed to be fully inclusive and to acknowledge the learning and achievements of pupils with the most profound difficulties in learning.

Although they are reported by QCA/DfEE (2001a) to be 'useful as one of several mechanisms for setting school improvement targets' (see Chapter 9), the P scales are not associated with any tests – their use relies upon the 'professional judgement' of teachers in the context of ordinary classroom activity. In terms of the curriculum, these materials can be used primarily:

- as source and reference materials for the development of subject-focused assessment opportunities in schemes of work;
- in support of day-to-day teacher assessment;
- to enable staff to record and report upon progress and achievement over the course of a year or key stage.

As these related functions suggest, assessment for its own sake is of little value. Assessment should only be undertaken if the information gained is to be used – generally as an indication of progress or as a means of identifying areas for future development. Assessment in schools can be said, therefore, to have two main functions:

- Formative – whereby the information gained through assessment is used to inform planning, for individual pupils and groups or cohorts of learners, and to address continuity of learning.
- Summative – whereby an assessment is made, following a course of teaching, to see what learning has taken place and what has been retained by a pupil or group of pupils. Summative assessments can also be used in the monitoring, review and evaluation cycle in order to ascertain the effectiveness of teaching methods, resources and groupings.

Figure 8.3 shows how summative and formative assessment can be combined to assist with planning for continuity.

In the left-hand column in this example, there is a section that draws down, from the long-term and medium-term plans, what staff intended to teach in an English

Figure 8.3 The summative and formative functions of assessment

Subject **English**   Term **Summer**

Pupil **John Smith**

What will be taught?	What was covered?	What did he/she do?
Poetry First World War poets Sassoon, Owen, Brooke. *Lord of the Flies* Writing Eyewitness accounts, writing journalist reports of an event during the term. Using journalist accounts from First World War, examining language and looking at methaphors.	Examination of emotions in the war poets. Pupils wrote poetry in the style of one of the poets. Discussion of emotions and relationships carried on through work on *Lord of the Flies*. Some drama with pupils assuming roles based on the characters from the book. Extracts from newspapers used to examine journalist styles. Accounts written by pupils of summer fayre, sports events and theatre trips.	John listened to tapes of the war poets and answered questions onto tape. Demonstrated good understanding of vocabulary and was able to put poetry into context of time. Not able to write a poem, but suggested ideas which were written by another pupil. Made good verbal contributions to discussion on *Lord of the Flies*. Made a 'radio broadcast' of school fayre which was used during lesson discussion on different reporting media. Listened well to archive recordings from war and commented on these.

Individual objectives from annual review

To have the confidence to make greater verbal contributions in lessons.

To remain on task for periods of at least 30 minutes.

To use media other than written to express his ideas and to be prepared to share his ideas with others in class.

To participate in practical activities in lessons and to join in group activities.

Objectives addressed in the subject this term

John did make good contributions to discussions on *Lord of the Flies*, a story which he enjoyed. This was provided for him on tape and he clearly listened to all of it. Using tape recordings enabled John to work alone some of the time, but he was happy for these to be used in class and this gave him more confidence to participate in class. We have encouraged John to use tape recordings and in the journalism work this term have tried to help him to see that radio broadcasts are a valuable source of information. This did encourage him to use his limited reading skills in developing cues for his recordings. John still reluctant to join in practical parts of the lesson, preferring to work alone.

Forward planning

Next term we will be working on writing and producing a play. It will be difficult to encourage John to play a speaking role and may be best to encourage him to contribute ideas for the writing in a workshop situation.

unit of work. At the end of the term, a more accurate account of what was actually taught is written in the middle column. These notes may be used, in conjunction with curriculum plans, as a record of experience for the class. They will also be of some help to a subject co-ordinator (see Chapter 9) who needs to review the ongoing record to ensure appropriate coverage of the subject and who may wish to use notes like these to support the review and revision of schemes of work. On the right-hand side of the sheet, the responses and contributions of a pupil with special needs are recorded in relation to the term's subject coverage. Objectives set for the pupil through the annual review and individual planning processes (see Chapter 7) are set out across the centre of the sheet. Comments are provided on how these objectives were addressed during the term. The section on forward planning indicates how, in the coming term, the teacher will continue to address the individual needs of the pupil and build upon the work of the current term. This approach could, of course, be used in conjunction with the principles described earlier of negotiation with the pupil to ensure a common understanding of what is to be achieved. Equally, involving the pupil in self-evaluation related to the objectives set may play an important role in developing pupil confidence and ensuring clarity of purpose.

Many schools have begun to involve pupils in expressing their opinions related to the lessons they receive and their own performance and a great deal has been written about pupil self-evaluation in recent years. *Curriculum Guidance 9* (NCC 1992) provides examples of ways in which pupils could contribute to the assessment process. These range from simple statements about 'things I can do by myself' to the more sophisticated use of information technology to indicate how well a pupil feels she performs in a specific curriculum area. Hardwick and Rushton (1994) offer a number of examples of the ways in which pupils can be involved in developing their own records. Lawson's updated book on *Practical Record Keeping* (1998) includes a whole section on pupil involvement.

Consultation with pupils about their experiences and achievements has been recognised as an important process in many schools for a number of years. Pupils make valuable comments on their own progress and on their aspirations for future learning through end-of-year reports and often by attending parent consultation evenings. Pupils with special needs have equally valid contributions to make in this area and, with careful consideration of the media to be used to provide access, this can generally be achieved. In the following paragraphs, we consider these possibilities in more detail.

Records of achievement and experience

The involvement of pupils in learning and assessment procedures can provide a sound foundation for ensuring that they develop the skills that they will undoubtedly need to gain any level of independence or semi-independence in the post-school years. The provision of accredited pathways that recognise pupil achievement is critical in enabling pupils to gain their full entitlement to life in the wider society beyond school. In recent years, the expansion of accreditation schemes such as ASDAN (Award Scheme, Development and Accreditation Network) and Towards Independence has found favour with many schools concerned to support all pupils in leaving school with an appropriate qualification. Such schemes were well established in a number of special schools many years ago and are now equally often to be found being used within mainstream settings.

The provision of a record of achievement for every pupil became established practice in mainstream schools in the 1980s. Such an approach enabled pupils to take ownership of records of their own work, selecting examples of which they were particularly proud and building a portfolio which demonstrated a wide range of accomplishments. Good records of achievement practice recognised not only academic performance but could also indicate other areas of strength and achievement, such as awards for community work, sporting prowess or musical ability. In principle, the record of achievement folder could provide an overview of the accomplishments of an individual which would enable a prospective employer or a further education establishment to recognise the strengths demonstrated through the presentation of a broad and varied bank of evidence. The national Record of Achievement folder was made available for every pupil and many employers came to recognise the burgundy-coloured folders carried by pupils attending job interviews. These folders have been replaced in many settings by Progress Files. The terms 'achievement file' or 'record of achievement' are still preferred by many users working with young people with learning difficulties since they are seen to be more inclusive.

For pupils with special educational needs, it is essential that records of achievement become more than just a series of documents collected together in a file. The record should be a working document which is regularly updated, taking full account of the views of the individual pupil and seeking the guidance of teachers, other staff and families. School staff are not always aware of the achievements of pupils outside school and regular communication with parents and other carers may be essential to ensure that the record reflects the achievements of the whole pupil. School staff should work with pupils to ensure that records of achievement are well annotated. It is easy to assume that anyone reading the record will be able to understand why specific pieces of work are included but this is not always the case. Simple annotation can enable the reader to understand exactly what a pupil has achieved; the significance of the record provided; and why a particular piece of work has been included in the file. Some schools have developed simple proforma to enable this to be managed consistently.

Figure 8.4 takes the role of the pupil in self-evaluation beyond the simple 'I can' statement by including two further elements. Firstly the 'I can' statement is qualified by clear criteria – 'I know I can do this because ...' Secondly, evidence is to be compiled which further supports the assessment. The pupil knows that she can complete the task described (in this case naming and sorting shapes) because she has recognised that an assessment was made of the task on two separate dates. In addition to this, the teacher has accumulated evidence to support the assessment and has discussed this with the pupil.

Lawson (1998) has emphasised that the processes of developing, collating and editing records of achievement should enhance learning. This will only be possible if schools make regular reference to the file to reappraise learning with pupils and to use the information to influence planning and target-setting processes. If records are to be meaningful to many pupils with learning difficulties, they will have to encompass more than text on sheets of paper. As is acknowledged by QCA/DfEE (2001a) and Lawson (1998), records, and particularly records of achievement, can include materials preserved in a range of media – photographs, video passages, tape sequences, samples of work, real objects, or digitally recorded and processed images, sounds and commentaries. These modes of recording can enhance the extent to which pupils and their peers are able to record their own comments, ideas and assessments and take these materials with them into planning and review meetings.

For some pupils, particularly those with profound and multiple learning difficulties or other complex needs, it may be important to maintain records of experience. The record of experience should comprise a file which not only demonstrates what

Figure 8.4 Pupil self-recording with staff annotation

Mathematics Self-Assessment

Pupil's name Amy Green

I can...

Name and sort the shapes

square

circle

triangle

I know I can do it because...

I did this without any help on 8 December and again on 4 February. Mrs Wells made a video recording of me doing it.

(Dictated to Mrs Jones 4 February)

Evidence collected

Work from Amy's maths books retained. Worksheets from school maths scheme also retained. Both assessment sessions were video recorded and discussed with Amy.

a pupil has done and experienced, but also provides an opportunity to review the education being provided. For pupils whose achievements may be measured in small increments, it is important that they gain recognition for their response to the learning experiences provided. Many schools have developed records of experience that make use of photographs. These are most useful when accompanied by detailed annotations that indicate why the pictures have been selected. For example, a photograph that shows a pupil sitting at the table during lunch-time may be of limited value. However, if this same photograph is accompanied by an annotation which states that *this photograph shows Michael taking food to his mouth using a spoon independently for the first time*, its value to the reader and as a record is considerably enhanced.

Principles for the management of records of achievement or experience should be established in all schools. These records should:

- be seen as the property of the pupil and, wherever possible, take full account of their opinions and decisions regarding content;
- be a celebration of the individual pupil;
- be regularly reviewed and updated;
- be used to inform planning and target setting;
- reflect the pupil's achievements and experiences outside as well as within school;
- be used to inform reports, with pupils selecting extracts to enable these to become a celebration of success.

Accreditation

The development of a broader range of accreditation opportunities to build upon the traditional examination routes can be seen to have had many benefits for students with special educational needs. Programmes such as *Moving On*, developed by EQUALS (a national support group for teachers of pupils with complex needs), have enabled all pupils to have their achievements recognised and have supported teachers in the development of materials which can be used for assisting pupils in the development of greater independence. Accreditation programmes such as ASDAN, which offer pupils opportunities to progress in a structured way through a hierarchy of skills, understanding and competencies, have provided teachers with a positive framework upon which they can base their planning for post-school life. In most schools, it is unlikely that one system of accreditation will be suitable for all pupils and it will be necessary for teachers to give careful consideration to how they plan for recognising pupil achievements and providing a structure for planning the later years of schooling. Schemes such as ASDAN have received recognition by national bodies such as the Qualifications and Curriculum Authority and have incorporated important opportunities for teachers to address key skills. However, the schemes alone are unlikely to provide the breadth and balance required for most students. Policy and planning should therefore ensure that key skills are implemented through and alongside other activities. Schools may wish to ask critical questions before embarking upon the use of any accreditation scheme. These questions may include:

- Are there other local schools using the scheme with whom we can share information and gain support?
- Does the scheme provide information and materials that are accessible to our pupils?
- How aware are local employers and further education providers of the schemes available?
- Is there a scheme that is being followed through in local further education provision in order to ensure a smooth transition from school?

It is important that accreditation schemes are not seen as separate from the main school curriculum that leads towards preparation for school leaving. Teachers need to be aware of the purpose of the curriculum in relation to preparation for adult life and to ensure that teaching in the earlier years relates well to and anticipates the skills, knowledge and understanding needed for working on the accredited programme.

Most programmes achieve success with pupils who have already been encouraged to take responsibility for some of their own learning and assessment procedures and who have been well prepared for the greater autonomy needed.

Closing comments

Throughout this chapter we have argued that pupils should play a full part in assessment, recording and reporting procedures. We have given examples of how this may be achieved. This philosophy, further reflected in other chapters of this book, builds upon the belief that education should be concerned with far more than the provision of skills and knowledge. It should develop independence and autonomy which cannot be achieved unless teachers enter into a partnership with their pupils (Tilstone 1991) and encourage them to take some responsibility for their own learning. These aspects of the tasks associated with assessment, recording and reporting are emphasised in the outline 'map' of assessment, integral to other curriculum and individual planning processes, we provide as Figure 8.5. School staff may wish to use this map in order to audit the assessment, recording and reporting processes they follow themselves and to review the extent to which pupils are involved at all stages. We take our discussion of the monitoring role further in the next chapter of this book.

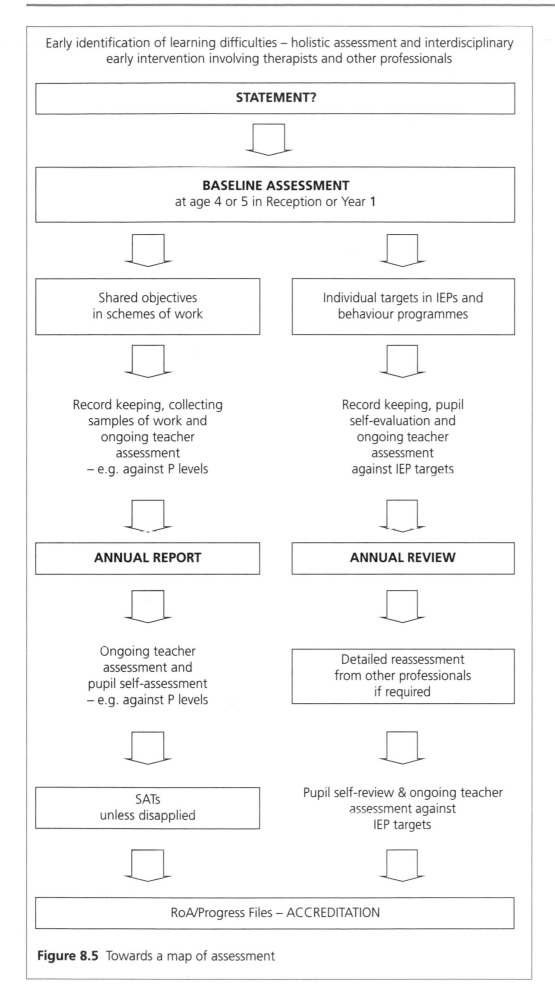

Figure 8.5 Towards a map of assessment

9 Monitoring and co-ordination

Subject co-ordinators often appear to face a daunting task in monitoring their subject throughout a school. In some schools this may require work across four key stages, with a broad knowledge of the content requirement this entails and an expectation that co-ordinators will keep up to date with all developments in their particular subject. In many primary and special schools with a small number of staff, teachers will carry responsibility for several subjects, thus multiplying the difficulties of maintaining a monitoring brief. To add to this seemingly impossible venture, the majority of subject co-ordinators, while being aware of the advantages of classroom observation or co-operative teaching as part of the monitoring process, have little or no non-contact time within which to manoeuvre.

In an ideal world, subject co-ordinators would spend time in classrooms observing their subject being delivered. They would pass on their expertise through team teaching and would have time to discuss their subject with teachers. They would provide assistance with planning and the development of teaching materials, and would still have time left over to co-ordinate resources. In the real world, co-ordinators are working with minimal time, have responsibilities for several aspects of school life and seldom have time to monitor what is happening in their subject. The Office for Standards in Education have made it clear that they consider arrangements for curriculum co-ordination and continuity to be an important issue (Ofsted 2003). Furthermore, with an emphasis upon assessing school effectiveness, the progress of individual pupils and the standards they achieve, it has become ever more important for subject co-ordinators to be able to provide clear evidence in all of these areas.

Farrell (2001) has emphasised the changing accountabilities that now exist in schools with a concentration of efforts upon ensuring that pupils are receiving their full curriculum entitlement and making progress at a pace that is matched to individual needs. He stresses the need for careful baselining that enables all staff to measure the progress of individuals and groups of pupils from a clearly established starting point. The demands for schools to set targets that enable them to make statements about their effectiveness have increased in the past few years (see below) and, as a result of this, subject co-ordinators in many schools have had to take on additional responsibilities.

The chapter will begin from the standpoint that teachers, while recognising the importance of curriculum co-ordination, have only a limited amount of time within which to fulfil this role. In so doing, a model will be presented which attempts to meet the requirements of curriculum co-ordination through practical tasks designed to gain information and promote curriculum development.

What is the purpose of subject monitoring?

In many special and primary schools, staff are required to have a generic expertise which would be regarded as preposterous in secondary schools. Prior to the introduction of the National Curriculum, teachers taught a range of subjects, often working with only limited expertise in some of these. The expanded content of the National Curriculum has increased the pressure upon teachers to have a more in-depth knowledge of the subjects they are teaching. In many instances, this has coincided with a reduction in the number of local authority advisory staff available to provide the necessary training and support which would have allowed for a more logical transition through this period of change. All too often, teachers have been left feeling isolated in their efforts to increase their expertise in a number of subjects and across several key stages. To expect teachers to continue working within a generic framework with little support is unacceptable. An early role for the subject co-ordinator must therefore be to establish credibility and expertise in a subject and to become prepared to pass their knowledge on to colleagues in the school (Sebba 1994). The role of subject co-ordinator as a support for colleagues is of paramount importance and needs to be carefully thought out if it is to be effective.

In assuming a subject co-ordination role, it is equally important to recognise that other staff have a responsibility in supporting the co-ordinator (see Chapter 3). Subject co-ordinators can have a tremendous and beneficial effect upon their subject in the school but, without the co-operation of all staff and the support of the management of the school, many of the benefits are unlikely to be realised. Having appointed co-ordinators, the managers and governors of the school have a duty to provide them with support in fulfilling their roles. There should also be an obligation upon all staff to provide the information and co-operation necessary to enable co-ordinators to perform effectively.

Monitoring should be used as a means of supporting staff in curriculum delivery. It should ensure that pupils receive the broad, balanced, relevant and well-differentiated curriculum that has become the touchstone of education in recent years. Monitoring must focus upon curriculum coverage, pupil achievements and quality of teaching. It must provide opportunities for the non-specialist teacher to gain confidence and develop the skills that will enable them to teach subjects more effectively. It should also provide indicators for the co-ordinator of areas that require further development or adjustments to resourcing. Monitoring should be a collaborative process in which staff are fully involved with the co-ordinator in making decisions about adjustments to teaching or ways in which the curriculum may move forward.

Monitoring – 'I just don't have the time'

How, then, can the subject co-ordinator with minimal time be effective in monitoring the curriculum? Accepting that there is no real substitute for spending time in every class observing teachers, but that this may be impossible in practical terms, we must look for approaches that will gather information consistently and achieve a balanced and manageable approach.

Tangible evidence related to the effectiveness of subject management and delivery can be obtained through a range of sources that can be examined outside the classroom. These include teacher plans, teacher records, pupils' work and reports. In order to be effective in gathering information, it is essential that subject co-ordinators

Table 9:1 Key questions for monitoring

QUESTIONS	SOURCES OF INFORMATION
KEY: PW = Pupil's work, TR = Teacher records, TP = Teacher plans, R = Reports	
Is curriculum balance being achieved? Are pupils receiving their entitlement to all parts of the subject?	**PW, TR, TP, R**
Are teachers recording pupil achievements and experiences?	**TR**
Is work being differentiated to meet the individual needs of pupils?	**TP, TR**
Are teachers using a range of teaching approaches?	**TP**
Are requirements for reporting the subject being met?	**R**
Is there continuity between classes in each key stage?	**TR, TP**
Is there progression in planning and delivery through the key stages?	**TP, TR**
How good is teacher understanding of the subject?	**TP, PW**
Are teachers using appropriate resources for curriculum delivery?	**TP**
Are teachers consistent in their judgements about pupil progress?	**PW, TR**
Are targets set through annual review being addressed and met?	**PW, TR, TP, R**

are clear about what they are seeking. The grid provided in Table 9.1 gives a list of key questions that co-ordinators may wish to ask about their subject and indicates where some of the answers are likely to be found.

All of the evidence gained through this approach comes from documentary materials which can be examined at a time that is of greatest convenience to the co-ordinator and the class teacher. The grid does not provide an exhaustive list of questions, but rather gives an indication of some of the enquiries that a co-ordinator may make and the sources of information that may be used to provide answers. Subject co-ordinators will wish to add to or subtract from this list, depending on the current position of their school and of their subject.

Examination of documentary evidence is not sufficient in itself as a way of monitoring a subject. Other strategies need to be deployed which provide a systematic way of asking questions, interpreting information and taking action to move a subject forwards. Building upon the grid provided in Table 9.1, one means of developing subject co-ordination is through the use of what may be termed a 'curriculum monitoring diary' approach.

Using a curriculum monitoring diary

Any examination of curriculum documentation or pupils' work needs to be systematic and manageable. The use of a curriculum monitoring diary is one approach that

Figure 9.1 Curriculum monitoring diary – worked example

CURRICULUM MONITORING DIARY		TERM **Summer**
CLASS **5 (KS2)**	TEACHER **Miss Willis**	SUBJECT **Art**

WORK UNDERTAKEN DURING THE TERM

Investigating and making
Still life drawing and painting of artefacts from history study unit on the Romans.
Mosaic collages of Roman floors.
Fabric printing – Roman designs on cotton for ceremonial togas.
Pottery – Roman pots with scraffito designs.

Knowledge and understanding
Visit to museum to see the work of Roman potters.

PUPIL'S WORK SEEN

John Parsons: Drawings of Roman spear and sword in pencil, and other sketches in charcoal.

Elizabeth Carr: Coil pots with scrafitto design. Collage made with three other pupils.

Wasim Khan: Drawings in pencil of Roman helmet, and paintings of sword and spear.

TEACHER RECORDS SEEN
Records indicate all pupils receiving appropriate coverage through term's work.

Skills identified as focus during term – observation, choice and use of colours, and manipulative skills.

Observational drawing building upon work on buildings from last term. Miss Willis is using pupil sketchbooks as part of record, and has retained samples of pupils' work. All work retained is dated and annotated.

WORK PLANNED FOR NEXT TERM
All pupils move up to Mr Evans and will do a textiles course next term. Class split into two groups, one group to complete course each half-term.

Work planned – spinning and weaving with wool, using vegetable dyes for wool, tie dying, introduction to wax resist (batik).

Visit arranged to craft centre to see spinners, weavers and dyers at work.

Spinning and weaving equipment on loan from county resource centre.

Advisory teacher visiting twice (once for each group).

assists with this task and Figures 9.1 and 9.2 provide a format that can be used in this way. The format provided here is simple and demands that comments are kept short and focused. After completion, the diary should be used as the basis for discussion and review with the class teacher and as an indicator for any action to be taken. A particularly positive approach, should time allow, would be for the co-ordinator to complete the diary with the class teacher. In reality it is more likely that the subject co-ordinator will undertake this task alone.

The diary is used in the following way. The teacher examines documentary materials from a class, as indicated in Table 9.1, asking the questions and using the information obtained to complete the diary. In practical terms, the subject co-ordinator should not expect to see the work and records of every pupil in the class, but should consider establishing a curriculum monitoring rota (see Figures 9.7 and

---

Figure 9.2 Curriculum monitoring diary – blank format

CURRICULUM MONITORING DIARY   **TERM**
CLASS   **TEACHER**   **SUBJECT**

WORK UNDERTAKEN DURING THE TERM

PUPIL'S WORK SEEN

TEACHER RECORDS SEEN

WORK PLANNED FOR NEXT TERM

9.8), which will be explained in more detail later in this chapter. The curriculum diary collates information under four headings:

- Work undertaken during the term
- Pupils' work seen
- Teacher records seen
- Work planned for next term.

The boxes under these headings should be completed by the subject co-ordinator on the basis of the information gained from the documentary evidence.

After completion, this diary sheet should be used as the basis for discussion with the class teacher. Time is a valuable commodity and many teachers feel that too much of it is spent in meetings. It is therefore essential that any meeting arranged between a subject co-ordinator and the class teacher is used to maximum effect. Co-ordinators should arrange a time of mutual convenience with the teacher to discuss the findings collated on the monitoring diary sheet and to identify means of moving the subject

Figure 9.3 Curriculum monitoring interview sheet – worked example

CURRICULUM MONITORING INTERVIEW

SUBJECT Science   **DATE** 18 February   **CLASS** 4

As agreed, the monitoring interview for your class will take place on Weds. 4 March at 4.00 p.m.

During the meeting I would like to discuss some of the following ideas with you.

PLANNING AND DIFFERENTIATION
How is the new planning system going? Is it helping with planning for next term?
Can we look at planning for better inclusion of George in practical lessons?

ASSESSMENT, RECORDING AND REPORTING
Can we consider the requirements for the subject report to parents at the end of the summer term?

CURRICULUM CONTENT
Look together at the electricity and magnetism module to be taught next term. Any modifications needed to this term's module on animal homes?

RESOURCES
Were resources adequate for this term? Are there additional requirements for next term?

I would also like to show you some new software for the CD which has arrived and may be useful next term.

STAFF DEVELOPMENT REQUIREMENTS
Are you happy with the content of the three modules to be taught next year?
Do you need any training related to these, or to other science matters?

If you wish to discuss other matters, or particular pupils, or if you would like to see any specific materials or equipment related to the subject, could you please let me know as soon as possible. Thanks for your help.

forward. Figures 9.3 and 9.4 provide an example of a curriculum monitoring interview sheet that can help with this process. This sheet identifies areas to be discussed under five headings:

- Planning and differentiation
- Assessment, recording and reporting
- Curriculum content
- Resources
- Staff development requirements.

The sheet is completed on the basis of information gained and entered on the monitoring diary sheet. It identifies clearly the date and time of a meeting which has been mutually agreed and the issues that the subject co-ordinator wishes to discuss with the class teacher. It should be given to the class teacher, along with a copy of the monitoring diary sheet, in advance of the meeting, giving sufficient time for the class teacher to identify any issues or questions that he or she may wish to discuss.

During the meeting between the subject co-ordinator and the class teacher, the curriculum monitoring diary should form the basis of much of the discussion. It should not, however, preclude opportunities for the class teacher to raise other matters

---

Figure 9.4 Curriculum monitoring interview sheet – blank format

CURRICULUM MONITORING INTERVIEW

SUBJECT	DATE	CLASS

As agreed, the monitoring interview for your class will take place on _____ at ____
During the meeting I would like to discuss some of the following ideas with you.

PLANNING AND DIFFERENTIATION

ASSESSMENT, RECORDING AND REPORTING

CURRICULUM CONTENT

RESOURCES

STAFF DEVELOPMENT REQUIREMENTS

If you wish to discuss other matters, or particular pupils, or if you would like to see any specific materials or equipment related to the subject, could you please let me know as soon as possible. Thanks for your help.

---

related to the subject. This meeting may also be used as an opportunity to introduce new resources or curriculum materials and to discuss the needs of individual pupils.

The frequency of this process may vary according to the size of the school and the time available to staff. Where a subject co-ordinator is managing several subjects, it may be that the monitoring for a specific subject cannot be carried out frequently. It is also important that monitoring processes do not impede important developments in planning and implementing schemes of work (see earlier chapters). It is appropriate for schools to plan initiatives over time so that, while the focus in one subject or one aspect of a subject is on monitoring, the focus for other subjects or aspects of the curriculum may be upon planning, implementation or review. There should, however, be an intention to conduct a planned, phased cycle of monitoring processes to ensure that good practices are being maintained and that identified difficulties are being addressed. Ideally, the use of the monitoring diary and interview approach would be carried out each term, in relation to aspects of the core subjects, for example, in order that work from a greater number of pupils within each class could be examined.

Following the initial meeting and those held in subsequent terms, information should be retained which will inform an annual report on the subject (see Figures 9.5 and 9.6). In the example provided here, the subject co-ordinator has reported under six headings:

- Content and coverage
- Pupil progress

Figure 9.5 Annual subject monitoring report – worked example

ANNUAL SUBJECT MONITORING REPORT

SUBJECT Science   **CLASS** 7   **DATE** July

TEACHER John Phillips

CONTENT AND COVERAGE:
Three modules this year: Our Bodies, Change and Moving Parts. Coverage of programmes of study from three attainment targets. Coverage of investigative science built into modules. Pupils also completed a science skills course, learning how to use various pieces of science apparatus. Visit made to car factory as part of Moving Parts module.

PUPIL PROGRESS:
Teacher records show that most pupils made good progress through the year. Introduction of skills sessions appear to have improved pupils' performances in investigations. Consistent use of Makaton symbol program on PC has enabled Michael to take a more active part in written parts of lessons. Some pupils found the materials prepared for Change module very difficult, insufficient differentiation caused problems and exclusion of some.

PLANNING:
Planning improved in second half of year when approaches to differentiation were better established. Most planning now takes account of cross-curricular opportunities. We now need to concentrate on planning to ensure a wider range of teacher approaches.

ASSESSMENT, RECORDING AND REPORTING:
Assessment carried out at the end of each module. Tasks devised did not take enough account of providing access for Michael. Assessment tended to look largely at skills and knowledge, but not at application. Need to incorporate assessment into investigative approaches. New recording system is being consistently applied, and contributed well to end of year report.

RESOURCES:
Need to review resources for Change module. More books related to Moving Parts, particularly those with less text, would be useful.

ACTION TO BE TAKEN:
Review assessment procedures for pupils with special needs. Investigate resource needs. Consider a wider range of pupil self-evaluation methods – work with Jenny from class 4 and Clare from class 5 on this as they have similar concerns.

- Planning
- Assessment, recording and reporting
- Resources
- Action to be taken.

This report should provide an indication of the status of the subject in the class at the time of writing. The content of the report should be agreed between the subject co-ordinator and the class teacher. The action to be taken should be considered in

Figure 9.6 Annual subject monitoring report – blank format

ANNUAL SUBJECT MONITORING REPORT **SUBJECT**   **CLASS**   **DATE** **TEACHER**
CONTENT AND COVERAGE:
PUPIL PROGRESS:
PLANNING:
ASSESSMENT, RECORDING AND REPORTING:
RESOURCES:
ACTION TO BE TAKEN:

relation to needs in the subject elsewhere in the school and should be given a clear timetable.

As was stated earlier in this chapter, it would be unreasonable to expect a subject co-ordinator to examine the work of every pupil in every class through the monitoring diary process. Much will depend upon the time that the co-ordinator is able to give to this process and the support that can be given by the management of the school. The process of selecting which pupils' work and records will be monitored should be a matter for agreement with the class teacher. It is essential, however, that the work of a reasonable cross section of pupils is monitored each year. It may, for example, be advisable to sample a selection of three or four pupils who have very different needs. This would enable the subject co-ordinator to ask questions about differentiation and planning for a range of needs and should reveal evidence of how this is being achieved. Once the monitoring of work and records has been completed, the subject co-ordinator will need to record which pupils have been through this process and what was found. Figure 9.7 gives an example of a monitoring rota completed after the first term of this process; Figure 9.8 gives a blank version.

The curriculum monitoring diary approach we have described is illustrated in Figure 9.9. As stated earlier in this chapter, there is no real substitute for subject co-ordinators getting into class for observation and collaborative work. The system described here does not preclude the use of such approaches but should be seen as complementary to, and supportive of, any practical work that the subject co-ordinator can undertake in class.

SUBJECT MONITORING ROTA   MATHEMATICS

CLASS 4   **YEAR**   **TEACHER** Clive King

	AUTUMN			SPRING			SUMMER		
PUPIL'S NAME	Paul Sutton	Ryan Clarke	Sue Longford	Wendy Bush	Zaheer Hussein	Leisa Watts	Clare Wilson	Jacob Cohen	Nick Parks
PUPIL'S WORK	Checked 12/12 Work on ATs 2 & 3 Marked to date	Checked 12/12 All work on AT 2 Marked to date	Checked 12/12 Work on ATs 2 & 3 Marked to date						
TEACHER RECORDS	Checked 15/12	Checked 12/12	Checked 15/12 No records for AT 1						
TEACHER PLANS	Emphasis next term on ATs 3 & 4	Additional support to be provided by SEN co-ordinator on Tues	Continuing work on AT 2						
REPORTS	None this term	Report prepared for SEN review in Jan. Sent to parents	None this term						

ANNUAL MEETING WITH TEACHER   DATE   17 January

Comments

Discussed the need to give some attention to AT 1 and agreed to provide some ideas for second half of spring term. Good level of support being provided for Ryan, some extra help to be provided on Tuesdays by Sue Robbins. New GINN workbooks appear popular, need to review availability of resources for AT 4 and to ensure that Clive is familiar with range of software for data handling in summer term.

Figure 9.7 Subject monitoring rota – worked example

SUBJECT MONITORING ROTA								
CLASS YEAR TEACHER								
	AUTUMN			SPRING			SUMMER		
PUPIL'S NAME								
PUPIL'S WORK								
TEACHER RECORDS								
TEACHER PLANS								
REPORTS								

ANNUAL MEETING WITH TEACHER   DATE

Comments

Figure 9.8 Subject monitoring rota – blank format

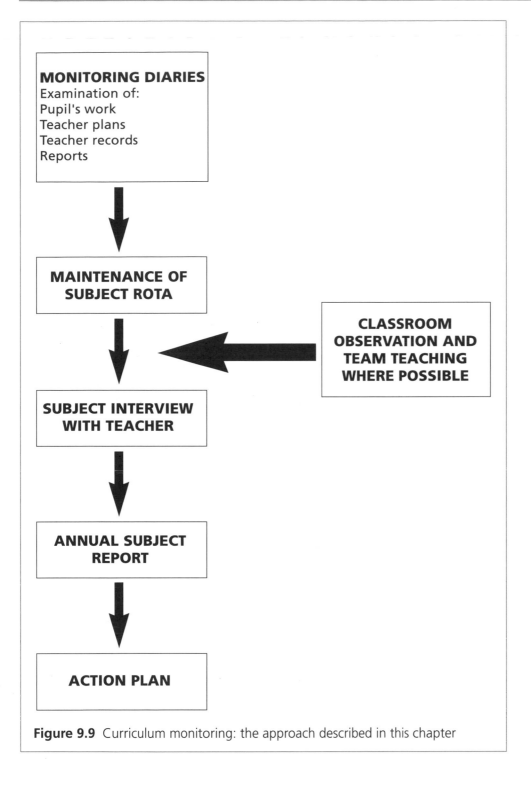

Figure 9.9 Curriculum monitoring: the approach described in this chapter

Further demands upon curriculum monitoring – whole-school target setting

Since the introduction of the National Curriculum, we have seen a new emphasis upon school accountability. Many Government initiatives have focused upon raising standards of achievement and encouraging schools to evaluate their own progress. Within this series of demands, a concentration upon target setting at individual pupil and whole-school levels has exercised the initiative of teachers concerned to ensure that pupils with special educational needs do not become marginalised by new expectations and procedures.

Supporting the Target Setting Process (DfEE/QCA 2001) indicates how schools may evaluate their own situations and establish targets for improvement through a phased cycle of school self-improvement. The document emphasises that the cycle should have two key elements:

■ using appropriate measures for overall pupil performance

■ setting targets to be achieved within specified timescales.

It also identifies four questions that schools might ask in relation to pupil achievement:

■ How well are we doing?

■ How do we compare with similar schools?

■ What more could we aim to achieve this year?

■ What must we do to make it happen?

These questions are intended to provide a catalyst for action on the part of schools and to lead to actions that enable schools to review their progress and identify targets for school improvement. It is inevitable that the senior management teams in schools will look to subject co-ordinators to provide them with a lead in relation to the targets to be set in specific curriculum areas. This places increased demands upon subject co-ordinators and makes the need for efficient processes and systems of monitoring ever more important. We will explore each of the stages in the school target-setting cycle in turn.

Stage 1 – How well are we doing?

This stage emphasises the need for schools to review their current situation and to gain a clear understanding of what pupils have achieved in relation to the curriculum provided. There is a recognition that targets set will fluctuate widely year on year because of differing cohorts of pupils and the different emphasis schools may give to specific curriculum subjects at specific times. It is also recognised that, in special schools, the focus may need to be on the progress made by individual pupils from established baselines rather than on cohorts of pupils or age-related factors. Effective schools will use this stage to ask questions not only about the progress made by pupils but also about the challenge of the individual targets that are set.

Stage 2 – How do we compare with other similar schools?

Identifying other schools of similar designation and population which also use similar measures of performance is essential. Use of the P scales or commercial packages such as B Squared or PIVATS is likely to be a key factor in collecting comparative data. However, schools will need to ensure an effective moderation process. It will be important to ensure that comparisons between pupil performances are made in carefully identified common curriculum areas using shared understandings of 'levelness'. Schools will need help with moderation and LEAs and central bodies have a critical role to play in this respect.

Stage 3 – What more should we aim to achieve this year?

Schools cannot be expected to address too many areas for development within a given year and it will therefore be essential that priorities are established on the basis of discussions with staff and governors. Targets should be closely allied to school development plans and will need to take account of staff needs and confidence. This will include a focus upon training and developing sufficient expertise before anticipating that progress will be made. It will often be necessary to set targets for specific groups of pupils, such as those with challenging behaviours, rather than across the school as a whole.

Stage 4 – What must we do to make it happen?

Schools will need to identify factors that will enable progress to be made. These may include the improvement of resources or accommodation. It will also be necessary to clarify and put into place strategies and procedures for monitoring, recording and moderating targets. Staff confidence will be increased only when systems are in place which support the making of accurate judgements.

Stage 5 – Taking action and reviewing progress

Clear guidelines with regards to the actions to be taken are essential. Responsibilities need to be identified along with key times and events in the year that may boost progress or be appropriate as times at which to collect data. Interim stages of assessing progress will enable staff to make modifications to existing procedures and support progress towards the final assessment of progress.

Some schools and LEAs have attempted to use this cycle to provide an indication of the actions that may be taken to develop whole-school target setting and to identify roles and responsibilities to enable improvements to be achieved. Figure 9.10 provides a summary of the key elements of this cycle and Figure 9.11 gives an example of how one school followed the whole-school target-setting cycle, in terms of targets, actions and responsibilities, across one year.

What enables effective target setting?

Planning, Teaching and Assessing the Curriculum for Pupils with Learning Difficulties (QCA/DfEE 2001a) should be seen as a key document in supporting schools in the self-assessment and target-setting process. It provides guidelines which:

■ Confirm the statutory entitlement to learning for all pupils and build upon the principles of inclusion set out in the National Curriculum.
■ Help schools develop an inclusive curriculum by:
 – setting suitable learning challenges
 – responding to pupils' diverse learning needs
 – including all learners by overcoming potential barriers to learning and assessment.
■ Provide a stimulus to revisit and revise existing schemes of work or to develop new ones. (p. 4)

These guidelines also suggest that schools may use the performance descriptions, or P scales, contained within the accompanying subject-specific booklets to support whole-school target setting. There are, however, some important considerations to be taken into account when using the P scales for these purposes:

■ The P scales do not provide a full description of what pupils might achieve and do not constitute a full and sufficient assessment system.
■ They provide a framework against which pupil progress can be measured in detail using the school's own assessment procedures.

- The P scales do not replace assessment materials contained in other developed schemes but should be viewed as complementary to these.

- They can provide a common language and a basis for comparison between schools only where schools take full account of variables in individual school populations.

We would caution schools to remember a further series of principles that will help to make whole-school target setting effective and meaningful for schools rather than an empty bureaucratic exercise:

- Remember that setting targets cannot, by itself, raise standards.

- Create a supportive environment for staff.

- Ensure that staff are not overwhelmed by targets.

- Provide focused training for all staff.

- Make a clear audit of resources to ensure that targets can be realistically addressed.

- Provide a sound evidence base for planning targets.

- Make targets SMART – specific, measurable, achievable, realistic and time-related.

- Set targets over a realistic time period – two years may be more appropriate than one for many targets.

- Ensure that senior managers play a role in both assessment and delivery of targets.

- Undertake regular monitoring and, on the basis of this, carry out legitimate modification of targets.

- Pursue collaboration between schools at all stages of the process, not only during assessment – this will increase understanding and assist in moderation.

The collection of data about the attainments of pupils with special educational needs is relatively undeveloped. Whether this process will enable effective comparisons of progress to be made between schools remains uncertain. The P scales may provide a useful common tool to enable this to happen, though just how instructive these comparisons will be is unlikely to be clear until several years of data collection have taken place.

Further demands upon curriculum monitoring – taking a more holistic view of pupil progress

The subject booklets associated with QCA/DfEE's *Planning, Teaching and Assessing the Curriculum for Pupils with Learning Difficulties* provide an essential aid to all subject co-ordinators in fulfilling their monitoring responsibilities. These documents place a renewed emphasis upon the need to value the progress made by all pupils within subjects. However, the guidelines emphasise that, for pupils with learning difficulties, the school curriculum should also embrace some important aims for pupils' learning across and beyond subjects. According to QCA/DfEE (2001a), the school curriculum should aim to:

- enable pupils to interact and communicate with a wide range of people;
- enable pupils to express preferences, communicate needs, make choices, make decisions and choose options that other people act on and respect;
- promote self-advocacy or the use of a range of systems of supported advocacy;
- prepare pupils for an adult life in which they have the greatest possible degree of autonomy and support them in having relationships with mutual respect and dependence on each other;

- increase pupils' awareness and understanding of their environment and of the world;
- encourage pupils to explore, to question and to challenge;
- provide a wide range of learning experiences for pupils in each key stage suitable for their age. (pp. 6–7)

There is clear and unambiguous recognition here of the fact that providing pupils with a breadth of subject knowledge and understanding is not the only purpose of schooling. The curriculum should also be a vehicle for the development of independence, autonomy and socialisation. When coupled with the affirmation of citizenship and the greater emphasis placed upon personal, social and health education in the revised National Curriculum, these aims provide teachers with an opportunity to address specific and individual needs within a whole curriculum model.

The implications for curriculum co-ordination are clear. Subject co-ordinators should pay attention not only to the progress that pupils make in terms of subject content, but also to the development of the individual as a learner in the context of each subject. It may be, for example, that a pupil is making slow progress in mathematics but, during the course of his mathematics lessons, has made excellent strides in his ability to socialise with others in the class and to take responsibility for his own equipment.

If comparisons between schools are to be made, they should take account not only of understanding and attainment within subjects, but should also adopt a holistic approach to viewing the impact of the school upon the pupil as a learner and a person. Subject co-ordinators will perform a particularly useful function if they are able to provide evidence related to the responses that pupils are able to demonstrate in applying learning in a range of contexts, managing their own learning needs and presenting a well-adjusted approach to gaining greater social independence.

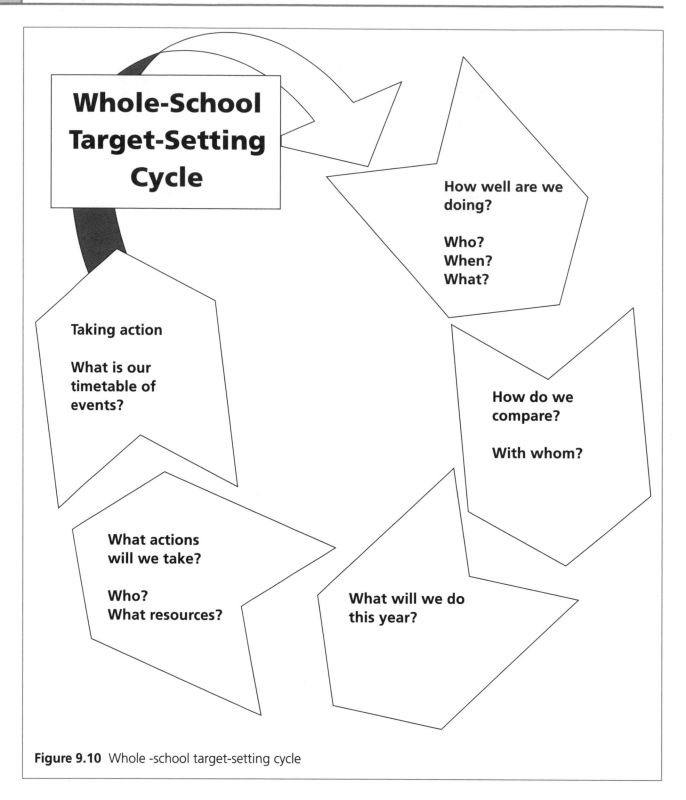

Figure 9.10 Whole -school target-setting cycle

Figure 9.11 Whole-school target-setting cycle (example)

Stage 1 How are we doing?	Actions	Responsibilities	When?
Assessment information from previous years collated	Class assessment records to be collected and entered on school spreadsheet	Assessment co-ordinator to gather information	March
Priorities matched to school development plan	School development plan to be reviewed	Governor's curriculum committee	April
Priority target areas for next year identified	Staff opinions to be sought regarding areas of the school development plan to be addressed	Time given at staff meeting	April

Stage 2 Compared to other schools	Actions	Responsibilities	When?
Identify schools for compilation of comparative data	Discuss our priorities with heads of other schools	Head teacher	May
Prepare information for baseline and to measure progress over past year	Compile P scale charts for pupils in selected curriculum area for development	Assessment co-ordinator	May
	Identify parallel groups in two other schools within the LEA (visit schools and discuss with appropriate staff)	Head teacher & assessment co-ordinator	May

Stage 3 Achievement this year	Actions	Responsibilities	When?
Discuss chosen area for development with staff	Use training day morning for discussion of strengths and weaknesses within subject	Deputy head to arrange training day	May
Identify specific groups of pupils for comparative exercise	Use afternoon for identification of groups of pupils and to begin target setting	All staff to bring class records and pupil files	
Set targets			

Stage 4 Making it happen	Actions	Responsibilities	When?
Identify resource needs	Review resources in chosen area	Deputy head	June
Identify additional staff training needs	Order any necessary new resources		July
	Plan staff training sessions (including September training day)	Subject co-ordinator of chosen area	June
	Present targets to governors	Head teacher	July meeting

Stage 5 Action and review	Actions	Responsibilities	When?
Provide staff training	Training day beginning of September	Deputy head	Sept
Targets in place	Introduce any new resources	Subject co-ordinator	Sept
Review progress	Review teacher records	Head teacher & assessment co-ordinator	1/2 termly
Visit from moderators			
Share information with other schools and governors	Attend moderator training	Assessment co-ordinator	November

10 Meeting the challenge

> If you'd said to me a few years ago that I'd ever be teaching *Romeo and Juliet* or *Julius Caesar* to my kids, I'd have laughed. I mean, for English we'd mainly been worrying about whether they could fill in an application form or read the destination board on a bus. But now that I'm doing Shakespeare, I wouldn't stop. It's shown us what the kids can do if you give them the chance. And there's so much in it for them – not just the language and the heritage stuff, but real, relevant ideas. It gets us into discussions that are about their lives as well as about Shakespeare's characters – about families and difficulties with your parents and about power and corruption – great ways into a lot of the material we need to cover for the older students in personal and social education. So, yes, this is one bit of the National Curriculum I'd want to hang on to – it's been brilliant.
>
> (English co-ordinator in a special school)

When the National Curriculum was first introduced, there was a considerable amount of debate about whether its influence should be seen as positive or negative (Sebba and Fergusson 1991; Sebba and Byers 1992). It has been our contention in this book that the National Curriculum has become firmly established as a significant but not all-encompassing part of the framework of the whole curriculum for all schools. Many teachers, like the English co-ordinator in a school for pupils with moderate learning difficulties we cite above, have positive things to say about the efforts they have made to provide access for their pupils to a curriculum that is now seen as an entitlement. It is encouraging, for instance, to debate the development of sex education programmes within the science and PSHE schemes of work in schools for pupils with profound and multiple learning difficulties or to observe classes of pupils with severe learning difficulties participating meaningfully in highly successful and clearly enjoyable modern foreign language lessons. Again and again, teachers who have approached the challenge of access to the National Curriculum honestly and imaginatively say that, despite their doubts and misgivings, they now set great store by classroom activities that they might otherwise not have dreamed of attempting.

These initiatives are not perceived as successful because they are part of the National Curriculum, because school inspectors seek to grade them as evidence of school effectiveness or even because local employers feel that they make the workforce more efficient. So what is the nature of the enthusiasm which is tangible among many teachers working with pupils with special educational needs? Why, in spite of the enormity of the workload and the frustrations over shifts and turns in policy, have many teachers decided that the National Curriculum is, in many ways, a force for liberation and emancipation rather than the restrictive influence that was once feared?

School autonomy

We have argued, in Chapter 1 of this book, that the National Curriculum can no longer be characterised as an overbearing and unwelcome invader upon curriculum development territory, pushing aside other indigenous priorities. The National Curriculum has been trimmed down to a size where it can be adopted as part of the framework of the whole curriculum without jeopardising the well-being of other aspects of school life, as we emphasise in Chapter 2. Schools' own priorities, whether these are revealed in physiotherapy sessions or adventurous outdoor activities, are to be seen as an important expression of the unique characteristics of different school communities. Schools are encouraged to develop their own curricula around the statutory foundations and to make them individual in terms of content and structure by linking them firmly to the needs of the schools' pupils.

We believe that it is appropriate for school communities to take this opportunity for autonomy very seriously. As we have argued before (Byers and Rose 1994), schools should be making their own decisions within the parameters of a properly constituted common framework. Part of the spirit of enthusiasm we report is due, we believe, to a resurgence of self-confidence in schools – a sense that it is possible for schools to return to defining, to a large extent, their own agendas for development. One of the useful outcomes of the system of school inspection is that schools can use the Ofsted criteria and benchmarks, alongside other strategies, as a tool for self-review and 'evaluating themselves' (Ofsted 2003). As Chapter 3 argues, the planning cycle, which moves from policy-making, through implementation towards review and revision, should be defined and managed by school communities. The school that sets its own agenda; its own targets; its own criteria for judging progress; and its own pace of change is in accord with the spirit of the times and will reap its own rewards. Among these rewards, we would argue, is the sense of common purpose which comes with shared endeavour, joint responsibility, co-operative ownership and teamwork. As we have emphasised, developments that are driven by pressure from the heavy hand of management, wielding the threat of external accountability, will be superficial, short-term and ineffective. A collegiate approach, characterised by clarity of intent, consensus and a fair and reasonable workload for all, is much more likely to bring about deep and long-lasting progress which is of real benefit to the whole-school community.

It is one of the central contentions of this book that this is the best way to work – indeed, that many stages in curriculum planning require collaboration at various levels in order to be meaningful. The task of negotiating breadth and balance within the whole curriculum (see Chapters 2 and 3) should involve the widest possible representation from the whole-school community – staff, governors, parents, pupils and other professionals. The development of units of work should be conducted at a departmental or key stage team level, with the input of subject co-ordinators in a supporting role (see Chapters 4 and 5). Assessment and record keeping can involve pupils as well as parents and members of staff (see Chapters 6 and 8). Information collected by individual subject co-ordinators in auditing and monitoring their subjects at different levels needs to be considered in a wider forum (see Chapter 9). Many schools have created departmental or key stage teams who, in addition to their responsibility for developing schemes of work, consider and act upon issues raised through review and evaluation. As the *SEN Code of Practice* (DfES 2001a) suggests, even short-term target setting can be enhanced where class teachers or pastoral tutors work closely with pupils, colleagues, other professionals and parents (see Chapter 7).

Another major theme of this book is that curriculum planning is a phased development task that takes time and never reaches a 'finished' state. It leads rather to a continuous cycle of review and development which, in close relation to the staff development plan and within the school development plan, is steered by the whole-school curriculum development plan.

Changing practice

Curriculum development can never be reduced to a paper exercise, however. Although much of this book describes a process of documenting innovation, we would assert that writing up schemes of work is meaningless unless changes in policy and documentation are reflected in revitalised classroom processes. In opening this chapter with the enthusiastic words of a teacher, we mean to celebrate the expertise that exists; to emphasise that innovation is driving positive change; and to encourage schools to focus their efforts on offering pupils better teaching and improved learning opportunities. The countless wheelbarrow loads of slick documentation that are carted away for pre-inspection analysis are worth nothing if practice at the interface between teachers and learners does not move forward.

Of course, practice is moving forwards – and this is the main reason why we have been motivated to collect together some examples of ways in which schools set their work down on paper. Improving practice is also the major motivating force that drives schools to continue to devote time, energy, commitment and enthusiasm to curriculum development work at a time when experience might have led to demoralisation. Teachers value the sorts of developments we have described above because they touch the lives of pupils in relevant, purposeful ways. Returning to the illustrations we gave earlier in this chapter, it is important for all young people to have an awareness of their bodies and their sexual selves, just as learning about culture and communication in France means a great deal to young people who may go there on holiday and who are aware that their brothers and sisters study the same language in their schools.

Entitlement to content

The recognition that pupils with special educational needs have an entitlement to content of this sort is, in itself, important. In many instances, the National Curriculum has encouraged schools to look beyond a narrow, utilitarian curriculum and has opened up new horizons in terms of the skills, knowledge, understanding and experience that might be offered to pupils with special educational needs of all kinds. We are firmly convinced that the re-evaluation and review that have gone on with regard to the curriculum for pupils with special educational needs in recent years have been timely and productive and that they should continue. The programmes of study for the subjects of the National Curriculum, together with religious education and the cross-curricular elements, have broadened the curriculum provided for pupils with special educational needs. As we noted in Chapter 1, important modifications made in the interests of inclusion helped to shape the launch of the revised National Curriculum in 1999 (DfEE/QCA 1999a, 1999b). Responsibility for managing balance in the whole curriculum is now firmly located in schools. It is an appropriate sense of balance, tempered by a clear sense of relevance in the light of pupils' needs and best interests, which makes entitlement to breadth a liberating possibility rather than a looming threat of overload.

Flexibility of access

The structural changes in the revised National Curriculum are hugely significant. The freedom that schools have to move around within the programmes of study, treating some aspects 'in depth' and others with a 'lighter touch' (QCA/DfEE 2001a) while selecting material that is developmentally appropriate from among the key stages, represents a great gain. The routes to access are now open although this does not diminish the task of making that access a practical reality. Extending access and probing the programmes of study for further areas that can be meaningfully taught to wider groups of pupils will be an ongoing challenge. As we have sought to demonstrate in this book, many schools are engaged in this process, revitalised by the knowledge that decisions about modes and levels of access are properly taken within school communities.

Part of this discretion is exercised in finding school-specific solutions to the challenge of curriculum design and management. In many places through this book we have presented alternative, equally valid ways of moving forward. Whether schools choose to proceed with long-term plans for units of work, with modules or with integrated schemes of work, pupils hopefully experience a variety of approaches to teaching. For them, the increase in exploration, problem solving and active enquiry that accompanies wholehearted attempts to implement the National Curriculum brings new opportunities to learn how to learn. This book has looked briefly at some of the issues arising from co-operative group work, or from pupil involvement in review and evaluation. We hope that initiatives like these, which bring another perspective regarding balance and variety to the classroom, will continue and prosper.

Inclusion

As all of the above suggests, we would argue that a curriculum for all, emphasising inclusion rather than separation, is a practical possibility. Many of the examples of good practice that we have cited in these pages have cross-phase implications and can be applied in a wide range of situations. This is not to argue simply for locational inclusion. There are pupils with special educational needs attending mainstream schools who find themselves marginalised and patronised, given the role of observer on the periphery of activity, rarely participants at the heart of what is going on. This, in our view, does not constitute inclusion simply because it takes place on a mainstream campus. At the same time, staff in special schools are breaking down separatist streaming structures and focusing upon curriculum development initiatives that emphasise differentiation, access for all and inclusion. We value the work of these colleagues very highly and hope that their example in developing inclusive teaching and learning will inform strategic planning towards structures and practices that can make inclusion in the mainstream meaningful. Staff in mainstream and special schools need to work together on the task of making inclusion work – and the development of the inclusive curriculum should be at the core of this process.

Concluding remarks

We are convinced that the National Curriculum has, in many senses, been a positive influence and a force for liberation and emancipation for pupils with special educational needs and their staff alike. We do not underestimate the enormity of the tasks that all schools have faced. However, although the timescale for innovation has been hectic and the messages often confused, we suggest that an opportunity for assimilation, consolidation and steady progress has arrived. Models for development, which have emerged painfully and uncertainly under the pressure of torrents of legislation, can be applied with more confidence and dignity to new subjects or to other aspects of the curriculum. Working with less haste will mean that more attention can be paid to the quality of innovation. As we have stressed, a phased programme of development will, over time, encompass the review and evaluation of policy and practice.

We are grateful to all the schools whose work is represented in these pages and hope that this book contributes to a growing sense of self-confidence in other school communities, founded upon purposeful curriculum planning.

References

Ainscow, M. (1989) 'How should we respond to individual needs?', in Ainscow, M. and Florek, A. (eds) *Special Educational Needs: towards a whole school approach*. London: David Fulton Publishers.

Ainscow, M. (1999) *Understanding the Development of Inclusive Schools*. London: Falmer.

Ainscow, M. (2000) 'Reaching out to all learners', in Daniels, H. (ed.) *Special Education Re-formed*. London: Falmer.

Alexander, R., Rose, J. and Woodhead, C. (1992) *Curriculum Organisation and Classroom Practice in Primary Schools*. London: HMSO.

Ashdown, R., Carpenter, B. and Bovair, K. (1991) 'The Curriculum Challenge', in Ashdown, R., Carpenter, B. and Bovair, K. (eds) *The Curriculum Challenge*. London: Falmer.

Babbage, R., Byers, R. and Redding, H. (1999) *Approaches to Teaching and Learning – including pupils with learning difficulties*. London: David Fulton Publishers.

Bennathan, M. (1996) 'Listening to children in schools: an empirical study', in Davie, R. and Galloway, D. (eds) *Listening to Children in Education*. London: David Fulton Publishers.

Berger, A., Morris, D. and Portman, J. (2000) *Implementing the Numeracy Strategy for Pupils with Learning Difficulties – access to the daily mathematics lesson*. London: David Fulton Publishers.

Booth, T. and Ainscow, M. (2002) *Index for Inclusion: developing learning and participation in schools*. Bristol: Centre for Studies on Inclusive Education.

Byers, R. (1992) 'Topics: from myths to objectives', in Bovair, K., Carpenter, B. and Upton, G. (eds) *Special Curricula Needs*. London: David Fulton Publishers.

Byers, R. (1994a) 'Providing opportunities for effective learning', in Rose, R., Fergusson, A., Coles, C., Byers, R. and Banes, D. (eds) *Implementing the Whole Curriculum for Pupils with Learning Difficulties*. London: David Fulton Publishers.

Byers, R. (1994b) 'Teaching as dialogue: teaching approaches and learning styles in schools for pupils with learning difficulties', in Coupe-O'Kane, J. and Smith, B. (eds) *Taking Control: enabling pupils with learning difficulties*. London: David Fulton Publishers.

Byers, R. and Rose, R. (1994) 'Schools should decide ...', in Rose, R., Fergusson, A., Coles, C., Byers, R. and Banes, D. (eds) *Implementing the Whole Curriculum for Pupils with Learning Difficulties*. London: David Fulton Publishers.

Carpenter, B. (1992) 'The Whole Curriculum: meeting the needs of the whole child', in Bovair, K., Carpenter, B. and Upton, G. (eds) *Special Curricula Needs*. London: David Fulton Publishers.

Chesworth, S. (1994) 'Devising and implementing a cross-curricular school recording system', in Rose, R., Fergusson, A., Coles, C., Byers, R. and Banes, D. (eds) *Implementing the Whole Curriculum for Pupils with Learning Difficulties*. London: David Fulton Publishers.

Cooper, P. (1993) *Effective Schools for Disaffected Students*. London: Routledge.

Costello, P. J. M. (2000) *Thinking Skills and Early Childhood Education*. London: David Fulton Publishers.

Davie, R. and Galloway, D. (eds) (1996) *Listening to Children in Education*. London: David Fulton Publishers.

Davie, R., Upton, G. and Varma, V. (eds) (1996) *The Voice of the Child*. London: Falmer.

Davis, J. (2001) *A Sensory Approach to the Curriculum – for pupils with profound and multiple learning difficulties*. London: David Fulton Publishers.

Dearing, Sir R. (1993a) *The National Curriculum and its Assessment – an interim report*. York/London: NCC/SEAC.

Dearing, Sir R. (1993b) *The National Curriculum and its Assessment – final report*. London: SCAA.

DfE (Department for Education) (1993) *Education Act 1993*. London: HMSO.

DfE (Department for Education) (1994) *Code of Practice on the Identification and Assessment of Special Educational Needs*. London: DfE.

DfE (Department for Education) (1995) *The National Curriculum*. London: HMSO.

DfEE (Department for Education and Employment) (1997) *Excellence for All Children: meeting special educational needs*. London: DfEE.

DfEE (Department for Education and Employment) (1998a) *Meeting Special Educational Needs: a programme for action*. London: DfEE.

DfEE (Department for Education and Employment) (1998b) *The National Literacy Strategy – Framework for Teaching*. London: DfEE.

DfEE (Department for Education and Employment) (1999) *The National Numeracy Strategy – Framework for Teaching Mathematics from Reception to Year 6*. London: DfEE.

DfEE (Department for Education and Employment)/QCA (Qualifications and Curriculum Authority) (1999a) *The National Curriculum – handbook for primary teachers in England: Key Stages 1 and 2*. London: DfEE.

DfEE (Department for Education and Employment)/QCA (Qualifications and Curriculum Authority) (1999b) *The National Curriculum – handbook for secondary teachers in England: Key Stages 3 and 4*. London: DfEE.

DfEE (Department for Education and Employment)/QCA (Qualifications and Curriculum Authority) (2000) *Curriculum Guidance for the Foundation Stage*. London: QCA.

DfEE (Department for Education and Employment)/QCA (Qualifications and Curriculum Authority) (1998, revised 2001) *Supporting the Target Setting Process*. London: DfEE.

DfES (Department for Education and Skills) (2001a) *Special Educational Needs Code of Practice*. London: DfES.

DfES (Department for Education and Skills) (2001b) *SEN Toolkit – Section 5: Managing Individual Education Plans*. London: DfES.

DfES (Department for Education and Skills) (2001c) *Inclusive Schooling – children with special educational needs*. London: DfES.

DoH (Department of Health) (1989) *The Children Act*. London: HMSO.

Farrell, M. (2001) *Standards and Special Educational Needs*. London: Continuum.

Fergusson, A. (1994) 'Planning for communication', in Rose, R., Fergusson, A., Coles, C., Byers, R. and Banes, D. (eds) *Implementing the Whole Curriculum for Pupils with Learning Difficulties*. London: David Fulton Publishers.

Fletcher, W. (2001) 'Enabling students with severe learning difficulties to become effective target setters', in Rose, R. and Grosvenor, I. (eds) *Doing Research in Special Education*. London: David Fulton Publishers.

Galloway, S. and Banes, D. (1994) 'Beyond the simple audit', in Rose, R., Fergusson, A., Coles, C., Byers, R. and Banes, D. (eds) *Implementing the Whole Curriculum for Pupils with Learning Difficulties*. London: David Fulton Publishers.

Galton, M. (1989) *Teaching in the Primary School*. London: David Fulton Publishers.

Griffiths, M. (1994) *Transition to Adulthood – the role of education for young people with severe learning difficulties*. London: David Fulton Publishers.

Griffiths, M. and Davies, C. (1995) *In Fairness to Children*. London: David Fulton Publishers.

Hall, V. (1997) 'Management roles in education', in Bush, T. and Middlewood, D. (eds) *Managing People in Education*. London: Paul Chapman.

Hardwick, J. and Rushton, P. (1994) 'Pupil participation in their own records of achievement', in Rose, R., Fergusson, A., Coles, C., Byers, R. and Banes, D. (eds) *Implementing the Whole Curriculum for Pupils with Learning Difficulties* (Revised edition 1996). London: David Fulton Publishers.

Hargreaves, D. and Hopkins, D. (1991) *The Empowered School*. London: Cassell.

Hart, S. (1992) 'Differentiation – way forward or retreat?' *British Journal of Special Education*, 19 (1), 10–12.

Jelly, M., Fuller, A. and Byers, R. (2000) *Involving Pupils in Practice – promoting partnerships with pupils with special educational needs*. London: David Fulton Publishers.

Johnson, R.T. and Johnson, D.W. (1983) 'Effects of cooperative, competitive and individualistic learning experiences on social development', *Exceptional Children*, 49 (4), 323–9.

Latham, C. and Miles, A. (2001) *Communication, Curriculum and Classroom Practice*. London: David Fulton Publishers.

Lawson, H. (1992) *Practical Record Keeping for Special Schools*. London: David Fulton Publishers.

Lawson, H. (1998) *Practical Record Keeping – development and resource material for staff working with pupils with special educational needs* (Second edition). London: David Fulton Publishers.

Lewis, A. (1992) 'From planning to practice', *British Journal of Special Education*, 19 (1), 24–7.

MacNamara, S. and Rose, R. (1995) 'Children's management of their own learning – the QUEST project', paper presented at the International Special Education Congress: Birmingham.

Marland, M. (1996) 'Personal development, pastoral care and listening', in Davie, R. and Galloway, D. (eds) *Listening to Children in Education*. London: David Fulton Publishers.

McCall, C. (1983) *Classroom Grouping for Special Need*. Stratford-upon-Avon: National Council for Special Education.

McLaughlin, C. and Byers, R. (2001) *Personal and Social Development for All*. London: David Fulton Publishers.

Morgan, G. (1992) 'Empowering human resource', in Riches, C. and Morgan, C. (eds) *Human Resource Management in Education*. Buckingham: Open University.

Munby, S. (1995) 'Assessment and pastoral care, sense, sensitivity and standards', in Best, R., Lang, C., Lodge, C. and Watkins, C. (eds) *Pastoral Care and Personal-social Education*. London: Cassell.

NCC (National Curriculum Council) (1989) *An Introduction to the National Curriculum*. York: NCC.

NCC (National Curriculum Council) (1990) *Curriculum Guidance 3: The Whole Curriculum*. York: NCC.

NCC (National Curriculum Council) (1992) *Curriculum Guidance 9: The National Curriculum and Pupils with Severe Learning Difficulties*. York: NCC.

NCC (National Curriculum Council) (1993) *Planning the National Curriculum at Key Stage 2*. York: NCC.

Nind, M. and Hewett, D. (1994) *Access to Communication*. London: David Fulton Publishers.

Ofsted (1993) *Curriculum Organisation and Classroom Practice in Primary Schools – a follow up report*. London: HMSO.

Ofsted (2003) *Handbook for Inspecting Special Schools and Pupil Referral Units*. London: Ofsted.

Otten, L. (ed.) (1999) *A Curriculum for Personal and Social Education*. London: David Fulton Publishers.

Ouvry, C. (1991) 'Access for Pupils with Profound and Multiple Learning Difficulties', in Ashdown, R., Carpenter, B. and Bovair, K. (eds) *The Curriculum Challenge*. London: Falmer.

Pagliano, P. (1999) *Multisensory Environments*. London: David Fulton Publishers.

Preedy, M. (1992), *Managing the Effective School*. London: PCP.

QCA (Qualifications and Curriculum Authority)/DfEE (Department for Education and Employment) (2001a) *Planning, Teaching and Assessing the Curriculum for Pupils with Learning Difficulties – General Guidelines*. London: QCA.

QCA (Qualifications and Curriculum Authority)/DfEE (Department for Education and Employment) (2001b) *Planning, Teaching and Assessing the Curriculum for Pupils with Learning Difficulties – Developing Skills*. London: QCA.

Reid, K., Hopkins, D. and Holly, P. (1987) *Towards the Effective School*. Oxford: Blackwell.

Rose, R. (1991) 'A jigsaw approach to group work', *British Journal of Special Education*, 18 (2), 54–7.

Rose, R. (1994), 'A modular approach to the curriculum for pupils with learning difficulties', in Rose, R., Fergusson, A., Coles, C., Byers, R. and Banes, D. (eds) *Implementing the Whole Curriculum for Pupils with Learning Difficulties*. London: David Fulton Publishers.

Rose, R. (1999) 'The involvement of pupils with severe learning difficulties as decision makers in respect of their own learning needs', *Westminster Studies in Education*, 22 (4), 19–29.

Rose, R., Fergusson, A., Coles, C., Byers, R. and Banes, D. (eds) (1994, revised 1996) *Implementing the Whole Curriculum for Pupils with Learning Difficulties*. London: David Fulton Publishers.

Rose, R., Fletcher, W. and Goodwin, G. (1999) 'Pupils with severe learning difficulties as personal target setters', *British Journal of Special Education*, 26 (4), 206–12.

Rouse, M. (1991) 'Assessment, the National Curriculum and Special Educational Needs: confusion or consensus?' in Ashdown, R., Carpenter, B. and Bovair, K. (eds) *The Curriculum Challenge*. London: Falmer.

SCAA (1994) *Consultation on the National Curriculum: an Introduction*. London: SCAA.

SCAA (1995) *Planning the Curriculum at Key Stages 1 and 2*. London: SCAA.

SCAA (1996) *Planning the Curriculum for Pupils with Profound and Multiple Learning Difficulties*. London: SCAA.

Scott, L. (1994) *On the Agenda – sex education for young people with learning difficulties*. London: Image in Action.

Sebba, J. (1994) *History for All*. London: David Fulton Publishers.

Sebba, J. and Byers, R. (1992) 'The National Curriculum: control or liberation for pupils with learning difficulties?', *The Curriculum Journal*, 3 (2), 143–60.

Sebba, J., Byers, R. and Rose, R. (1993, revised 1995) *Redefining the Whole Curriculum for Pupils with Learning Difficulties*. London: David Fulton Publishers.

Sebba, J. and Fergusson, A. (1991) 'Reducing the marginalisation of pupils with severe learning difficulties through curricular initiatives', in Ainscow, M. (ed.) *Effective Schools for All*. London: David Fulton Publishers.

Slavin, R.E. (1988) 'Cooperative learning and student achievement', *Educational Leadership*, 46 (2), 31–3.

Southworth, G. (1993) 'School leadership and school development: reflections from research', *School Organization*, 13 (1), 73–87.

Stationery Office (2001) *The Special Educational Needs and Disability Act 2001*. London: HMSO.

Stevens, C. (1995) 'News from SCAA', *British Journal of Special Education*, 22 (1), 30–31.

Swing, S.R. and Peterson, P.L. (1982) 'The relationship of student ability and small group interaction to student achievement', *American Education Research Journal*, 19 (2), 259–74.

Tate, N. (1994) 'Target vision', *Times Educational Supplement*, 2 December.

Tilstone, C. (1991) 'Pupils' Views', in Tilstone, C. (ed.) *Teaching Pupils with Severe Learning Difficulties*. London: David Fulton Publishers.

United Nations (1989) *Convention on the Rights of the Child*. Brussels: United Nations General Assembly.

Wallace, B. (ed.) (2001) *Thinking Skills Across the Primary Curriculum – a practical approach for all abilities*. London: David Fulton Publishers.

West-Burnham, J. (1994) 'Strategy, policy and planning', in Bush, T. and West-Burnham, J. (eds) *The Principles of Educational Management*. Harlow: Longman.

Widget Software (1994) *Writing with Symbols*. Leamington: Widget.